The Flesh of Images

SUNY series in Contemporary Continental Philosophy
_____
Dennis J. Schmidt, editor

The Flesh of Images

Merleau-Ponty between Painting and Cinema

Mauro Carbone

Translated by Marta Nijhuis

Published by State University of New York Press, Albany

La chair des images: Merleau-Ponty entre peinture et cinéma
© Librairie Philosophique J. Vrin, Paris, 2011.
http://www.vrin.fr

© 2015 State University of New York

For information, contact State University of New York Press, Albany, NY
www.sunypress.edu

Production, Ryan Morris
Marketing, Anne M. Valentine

Library of Congress Cataloging-in-Publication Data

Carbone, Mauro, 1956– author.
   [Chair des images. English]
   The flesh of images : Merleau-Ponty between painting and cinema / Mauro
Carbone ; Translated by Marta Nijhuis.
       pages cm. — (SUNY series in contemporary continental philosophy)
   Includes bibliographical references and index.
   ISBN 978-1-4384-5879-3 (hc : alk. paper)—978-1-4384-5878-6 (pb : alk. paper)
   ISBN 978-1-4384-5880-9 (e-book)
   1. Merleau-Ponty, Maurice, 1908–1961—Knowledge—Painting.   2. Merleau-
Ponty, Maurice, 1908–1961—Knowledge—Motion pictures.   3. Painting.   4. Motion
pictures.   I. Nijhuis, Marta, 1983– translator.   II. Carbone, Mauro, 1956–
Chair des images. Translation of: III. Title.

   B2430.M3764C373313 2015
   121'.34—dc23   2015001352

10 9 8 7 6 5 4 3 2 1

Contents

Acknowledgments

The present book is the "other side" of my previous work *An Unprecedented Deformation: Marcel Proust and the Sensible Ideas* (Albany: SUNY 2010), which presented some elements for a new conception of ideas. This book, for its part, aims at contributing to a reflection on the current status of images precisely meant as the ideas' sensible side.

This is the reason why I would like to thank Denny Schmidt for also welcoming this work into his series. I am likewise proud and grateful to mention that my appointment to the Institut Universitaire de France helped to financially support the accomplishment of this publication project.

Initial versions of some of this book's chapters have previously appeared in collective works or journals. I would, hence, like to thank the translators of those versions and the editors of those works and journals. My gratitude also goes to other colleagues and friends, who have all played an important role in the development of this work: Dudley Andrew, Giovanna Borradori, Francesco Casetti, Donatella Di Cesare, Duane Davis, Galen Johnson, Len Lawlor, Matt Tugby, and Emmanuel de Saint Aubert.

This book is for Marta, for everything is ultimately thanks to her.

Introduction

The Flesh and the Thinking of the Visual Today

It is well known that the notion of "flesh" is at the very core of Merleau-Ponty's later reflection. However, what is often forgotten is that "flesh" is another name for the "element" he also calls "Visibility."[1] This latter term is in turn a most interesting one, for it seems to be chosen so as to avoid any references to either a subject or an object, and to gather together activity and passivity. Indeed, in the pages of *The Visible and the Invisible* interrupted by his sudden death, Merleau-Ponty writes that the element of "Visibility" belongs "properly neither to the body qua fact nor to the world qua fact," thus, because of it, "the seer and the visible reciprocate one another and we no longer know which sees and which is seen."[2] Moreover, by "Visibility" Merleau-Ponty does not simply designate the ensemble of visible things. In fact, to him the term also includes the lines of force and the dimensions suggested by visible things as their own interior and exterior horizon. Eventually, according to what he learned from de Saussure's linguistics, he conceives what is visible in a diacritical way, that is, not as things or colors, but rather as a "difference between things and colors, a momentary crystallization of colored being or of visibility."[3] The latter thus appears as a texture of differentiations, in which the visible is always interweaved with an invisible that is indirectly shown by the visible itself.

Hence, considering these characterizations, the element of "Visibility" appears, on the one hand, as a challenge toward the categories on which the Western philosophical tradition is based, and on the other hand, as the announcement of the opening of a new ontological perspective. Indeed, the being of Visibility is characterized as *horizon being*: "a new type of being, a being by porosity, pregnancy, or generality, and he before whom the horizon opens is caught up, included within it."[4] "The second and more profound sense of the narcissism"[5] that Merleau-Ponty distin-

1

guishes refers precisely to this new type of being, and to the experience of inclusion that allow us to glimpse it. Such a sense would be a sort of *desire* of the visible Being *to see itself*, which would thus make it envelop those particular visible beings that are also seers. In this sense, Merleau-Ponty can even affirm "there is a relation of the visible with itself that traverses me and constitutes me as a seer."[6] This thesis also shows how he conceived our corporeity *from the standpoint of the experience of the flesh of the world*—namely, the experience of "Visibility"—just as he had conceived the latter from the standpoint of the first.

For these and more reasons, the present writing is based on a double conviction. On the one hand, characterizing Merleau-Ponty's notion of "flesh" by that of "Visibility" allows us to avoid most misunderstandings related to the interpretation of the first. On the other hand, it allowed Merleau-Ponty himself to elaborate extremely innovative ontological notions, which can help us to consider philosophically some of today's most significant cultural phenomena.

Amid such cultural phenomena, our new relationship to images is emblematic. In fact, it is well known that the ongoing development of optical and media technologies keeps opening our existences to new forms of visualization and visual experience. This implies a new centrality of images, not only practically and professionally, but also theoretically. Precisely on this basis, since the 1990s, an "iconic (or pictorial) turn" (also called *ikonische Wende*) was evoked in our culture, imposing a renewed analysis of the contemporary status of images.

Indeed, the mutations at work in the images' status seem to evoke— and to invoke at once—a form of reversal of "Platonism." By developing the premises affirmed by Nietzsche's philosophy[7] and explored by modern art, such a reversal of Platonism could maintain a thinking that matches our time, whose main way of thinking so far remains a *simplified* version of Plato's philosophy. Merleau-Ponty alludes to this meaning of Platonism in a passage from his last essay on philosophy of painting, namely *Eye and Mind*, where he writes: "The word 'image' is in bad repute because we have thoughtlessly believed that a drawing was a tracing, a copy, a second thing."[8] Sure enough, most contemporary thinkers will not find it hard to agree with such a statement. However, the image is still often supposed to find its most proper characteristic in "*presentifying what is absent as such.*"[9] This constitutively takes us back to the experience of death, actual or symbolic as it may be. However, if the image is not "a second thing," if *it does not copy* a model (but rather *creates it*), it reveals being much closer to the experience of birth than to that of death. Hence, the image denounces the Platonism underlying the opinion that too willingly associates it with death.

More generally, if the image is not "a second thing," then it can no longer be qualified as a simple *figure of reference*, as I will try to show in certain passages of the present work. Indeed, the nature of such a reference gets complicated, and its structure multiplies and becomes so entangled that the "first thing" back to which that reference is supposed to lead—that is, the absence it is supposed to presentify—ends up being untraceable.

The counterpart of such a status of the image is that of seeing, according to the definition elaborated by Merleau-Ponty in the "Introduction" to *Signs*, which is coeval with the writings I mentioned so far: "To see is as a matter of principle to see farther than one sees, to reach a latent existence. The invisible is the outline and the depth of the visible. The visible does not admit of pure positivity any more than the invisible does."[10] In fact, if the image is not "a second thing," it is precisely because "[t]o see is as a matter of principle to see *farther*" than the presentification of the absent as such. As I will stress in the pages that follow, Merleau-Ponty goes so far as to call this *seeing farther* "*voyance*,"[11] explaining that this "*voyance*" "renders present to us what is absent."[12] Beware, though: the *voyance* consists in seeing "farther than one sees," in showing us the invisible as "the outline and the depth of the visible." Precisely for this reason, the *voyance* "renders present to us what is absent" not simply by *presentifying* it, but rather in *creating* it as a particular *presence* which, as such, *had never been present before.*[13] In my opinion, what Merleau-Ponty also calls "quasi presence"[14] should be understood in this way. That is to say, not as a weakened presence, but rather as "the pregnancy of the invisible in the visible,"[15] as an effective and insisting "latency"; in short: as the *"flesh of the imaginary."*[16] In fact, this happens because seeing "farther than one sees" is seeing *"according to, or with"* what one sees. I am referring to another formulation from *Eye and Mind* on which I will have the occasion to dwell: "I do not look at [. . .] [a painting] as one looks at a thing, fixing it in its place. [. . .] Rather than seeing it, I see according to, or with it."[17]

It is clear that the seeing Merleau-Ponty tries to characterize by this formulation is no longer conceived according to the *representative* model of the window, which has become dominant in the Western culture since the Renaissance.[18] I believe that the characterization he tries to provide is closer to a different model, fundamentally questioning our contemporary experience of images: namely, *the screen model*. The window model made us believe we could *fix* the visible "in its place," while the screen evidently *makes us see* "according to, or with it." This is the reason for

Merleau-Ponty's continuous interest in cinema, although until a few years ago such an interest had not been sufficiently taken into account. In the present work, I will thus insist on this Merleau-Pontian interest, having examined some so far little-known or even previously unpublished writings. Of course, in *Eye and Mind* Merleau-Ponty refers his formulation to paintings, but in this way *he figures out a general conception of vision.* Such a conception shall match our epoch, and it should thus be possible to generalize it, so as to affirm that we happen to see "according to, or with" the images filling our perception as well as our imaginary. Indeed, "this red is what it is only by connecting up from its place with other reds about it, with which it forms a constellation, or with other colors it dominates or that dominate it, that it attracts or that attract it, that it repels or that repel it. In short, it is a certain node in the woof of the simultaneous and the successive. It is a concretion of visibility [. . .] A certain red is also a fossil drawn up from the depths of imaginary worlds."[19]

Hence, the seeing "farther than one sees"—understood precisely as a seeing "according to, or with" what one sees—is underlaid by the efficient and insistent latency of a dimension which the later Merleau-Ponty often qualifies as "mythical," featuring some most peculiar spatio-temporal dynamics and unexplored ontological implications. In short: it is in this sense that the element he called "Visibility" can also be called "flesh." In fact, "[b]etween the alleged colors and visibles, we would find anew the tissue that lines them, sustains them, nourishes them, and which for its part is not a thing, but a possibility, a latency, and a *flesh* of things."[20] The characterization of "Visibility" as "flesh" nods to such a general conception of vision—each epoch has its own—and, through it, to an attempt to express the "relationship between humanity and Being"[21] at work in our time. Thus, it reveals a point of *view* whose exploration, comprehension and formulation are evidently not an individual's matter: "Such are the extravagant consequences to which we are led when we take seriously, when we question, vision. [. . .] We are, to be sure, not finished ruminating over them. Our concern in this preliminary outline was only to catch sight of this strange domain to which interrogation, properly so-called, gives access."[22]

It seems to me that precisely the "extravagant consequences" indicated by Merleau-Ponty are what the aforementioned "iconic turn" wills, for its part, to explore, understand, and formulate insofar as possible, objecting to the attempts to reduce these consequences to a "linguistic kind of propositional logic."[23] This is why this "iconic turn" could not help, on the one hand, acknowledging the iconic turn that the later Merleau-

Ponty himself had to undertake so as to get to such consequences, and, on the other hand, sharing the reasons of Merleau-Ponty's iconic turn.[24] In fact, only by prolonging the direction marked by these "extravagant consequences," can one end up wondering, as W. J. T. Mitchell does, "what do pictures *really* want?"[25] Indeed, it is by starting from "the second and more profound sense of the narcissism" I mentioned above—that is, the narcissism of the visible Being—that Mitchell can get to write that images "present not just a surface, but a *face* that faces the beholder."[26] Here just as there, we find the same reference to an "inversion" of the gaze revealing our belonging to the visible, on the one hand, and the kinship between the visible and the viewers, on the other hand. Besides, this *inverse*[27] reference can only be thought by considering the meeting as a dimension, in which the roles are not preestablished once and forever *before* the encounter itself. In a relationship thus conceived—as Merleau-Ponty explains referring to the painter—"inevitably the roles between the painter and the visible switch."[28] In such a relationship—we might add—images are therefore lightened up by their own desires. This leads us back to the seeing "according to, or with" the images, a formulation whose ontological implications may now be better appreciated. And if "this complex field of visual reciprocity is not merely a by-product of a social reality, but actively constitutive of it,"[29] then it should all the more question our philosophical tradition, whose distinctions and oppositions are much stronger than those reciprocities.

One of the partisans of the radical questioning between philosophy and the status of images today is Georges Didi-Huberman. And indeed, in my opinion, what he writes concerning the current aesthetic interpretations of the notion of aura in Benjamin should be read precisely in the light of such questioning: "It is clear now: what is lacking in the average aesthetic positions in order to approach the problem of the aura, is a temporal model capable of accounting for the 'origin' in a Benjaminian sense, or for the 'survival' in a Warburgian sense. In short: a model capable of accounting for the events of memory, rather than for the cultural facts of history."[30]

Although it is only sketched, there is in Merleau-Ponty the thesis, on which I will dwell in the pages that follow, of a *reciprocal precession of the vision and the visible*. This paradoxical thesis takes seriously into account "the extravagant consequences" of the interrogation of the vision, and, in my opinion, it constitutes a fundamental contribution to the formulation of the "temporal model" evoked by Didi-Huberman. This is why such a thesis may lead us to a deeper understanding of the question concerning the *presence* of images today. That is to say, that very question about which we can indeed affirm what Merleau-Ponty himself had claimed apropos of painting in *Eye and Mind*: namely, that it "scrambles all our categories,"[31] and with them, even the identity of philosophy.

Such is, in the whole of its complexity, the challenge that Merleau-Ponty had taken up, the very challenge that indeed we cannot help taking up ourselves.

Chapter One

Flesh

Toward the History of a Misunderstanding

Merleau-Ponty: Nature as Flesh

The notion of "flesh" appears simultaneously as most ancient and recent in the history of Western thought. In the twentieth century, such a notion mainly seems to occur in order to spell the possibility of a communication between our body and Nature, and to rescue both from the objectivity to which Cartesianism had tried to reduce them. More precisely, we might say that in the twentieth century the notion of "flesh" coincides with a preeminent attempt to name the possibility of a communication between the Husserlian conception of the body as *Leib*—that is, an experienced unity of perception and motion[1]—and Nature, conceived in terms of "an enigmatic object, an object that is not an object at all," as Merleau-Ponty explains echoing Husserl. In fact, as Merleau-Ponty highlights, Nature "is not really in front of us. It is our soil [*sol*]—not what is in front of us, facing us, but rather, that which carries us."[2] In the effective and concise terms of his last working note attached to the unfinished *The Visible and the Invisible*, Merleau-Ponty writes this as follows: "Nature as the other side of man (as flesh— nowise as 'matter')."[3]

As is well known, Merleau-Ponty was the first one who, in the twentieth century, explicitly claimed a philosophical value for the notion of "flesh," using it in order to illustrate a type of being, which "has no name in philosophy,"[4] since it is neither matter nor mind nor substance.[5] Rather, it is the *unitary texture in which each body and each thing manifests itself only as difference from other bodies and other things.* Indeed, to him the notion of "flesh" designates the common horizon where all beings belong. In that sense, such a notion may even appear older than its specifically Christian acceptation. In fact, Merleau-Ponty defines it by resorting to the pre-Socratic term "element,"[6] as well as to another pre-Socratic expression, which in fact Aristotle attributes to Anaxagoras: namely, ὁμοῦ ἦν πάντα.[7] Although such an expression literally means "all things were together," Merleau-Ponty significantly does not relate it to an *origin*, but to something "originating," which, he warns, "is not all behind us,"[8] but rather in perennial explosion.[9] To come across the phenomenon of reversibility calling for an "ontological rehabilitation of the sensible"[10]—"a reversibility always imminent and never realized in fact"[11]—Merleau-Ponty suggests simply turning back to the experience of the touched hand becoming touching, which Husserl describes in §36 of *Ideen II*. Indeed, by being sentient and sensible at once, our body is *fleshly akin* to the sensible world. A world to which the very same ontological status that is attributed to the body shall thus be acknowledged.

Husserl, the Earth, and the Flesh

It was a 1934 Husserlian manuscript that particularly urged Merleau-Ponty to acknowledge one of the most decisive consequences of such a rehabilitation of the sensible. Merleau-Ponty came across this manuscript already in 1939, when visiting the Husserl Archives in Louvain as a foreign scholar—the first one ever. The manuscript in question is usually recalled under the title "Umsturz des kopernikanischen Lehre," and has been translated in English as "Foundational Investigations of the Phenomenological Origin of the Spatiality of Nature."[12]

In the summary of one of his last courses at the Collège de France, Merleau-Ponty comments as follows about this manuscript: "Through mediation we must again learn of a mode of being whose conception we have lost, the being of the 'soil' [*Boden*], and that of the earth first of all."[13] This is the very "mode of being" through which we heard Merleau-Ponty characterizing Nature precisely as "our soil."

Thanks to this "mode of being," as Merleau-Ponty's commentary highlights, we shall learn that "there is a kinship between the being of the earth and that of my body [*Leib*] which it would not be exact for me to speak of as moving since my body is always at the same distance from me. This kinship extends to others, who appear to me as 'other bodies,' to animals whom I understand as variants of my embodiment, and finally even to terrestrial bodies since I introduce them into the society of living bodies when saying, for example, that a stone 'flies.' "[14]

On this basis Merleau-Ponty affirms the *cobelonging* of the sentient and the sensible to the same "flesh" that interweaves our body, the other's body, and the things of the world, and that envelopes them in a horizon of "brute" or "wild Being" in which the subject and the object are not yet constituted. In this horizon perception takes place, on the one hand, in the indistinction of perceiving and being perceived and, on the other hand, in its intertwining with the imaginary, namely, our capability to perceive the *presence* of the absent. Such a capability is witnessed by the *ubiquity* of our seeing: "I am in Petersburg in my bed, in Paris, my eyes see the sun."[15]

It is precisely such "flesh of the sensible," to which we all belong and in which we belong to each other, which makes each of our experiences *communicable* and sharable. Husserl suggested that the Earth, meant as our soil, is properly neither in motion nor at rest, but remains on this side of either, being the condition of possibility of both.[16] Similarly, the flesh appears as the condition of possibility of the communication of all experiences. In this sense, it remains on this side of any effective communication or lack of communication. This is why the "flesh of the sensible" widens as flesh of history, language, and even ideality. Indeed, ideality itself turns out to be inseparable from its *carnal* appearance, inseparable from the *flesh of the images of the world* by which it arose. In fact, ideality is constituted by those images as their excess, and it is precisely *through* their appearance that it manifests itself. In the same way, as Merleau-Ponty writes in *Eye and Mind*, "when through the water's thickness I see the tiling at the bottom of a pool, I do not see it *despite* the water and the reflections there; I see it through them and because of them."[17] This is how a programmatic intention was reasserted by phenomenology. Namely, that of conveying attention onto *appearing* (and therefore onto *becoming*) in order to reinstate them into *Being*, by complying with their paradoxical characteristic, as Husserl had exemplarily been able to do in his "Foundational Investigations of the Phenomenological Origin of the Spatiality of Nature."

Merleau-Ponty comes to the notion of "flesh" by thinking of our relationship with the world in the direction showed by what he calls the "shadow" of Husserl's thought, that is, the "unthought" that such reflection projects all around itself. However, at the same time, Merleau-Ponty is inclined to flag that the danger of *merely reversing* the relations between what lies on this side of an edge that keeps remaining metaphysical and what lies beyond it, can also be hidden in an idea advocated by Husserl. Such an idea is that of a *stratification* of experience whose truth would be directly proportional to its depth. Merleau-Ponty thus criticizes Husserl's intention of " 'unravelling,' 'disentangling' what is entangled," which is the flesh itself. He also highlights that "the relation between the circularities (my body-the sensible) does not present the difficulties that the relation between 'layers' or linear orders presents."[18] In my opinion, it is to follow these circularities that the later Merleau-Ponty conceives the flesh starting from the body as well as the body starting from the flesh. This is particularly evident where he characterizes the flesh as visibility.

Franck, Nancy, Derrida: Body and Flesh

In the 1980s, proceeding in the speculative direction opened by Merleau-Ponty, Didier Franck proposed to generalize the translation of the German *Leib* by using the French term *chair*, that is, "flesh." In doing so, he first referred to Husserl's phenomenology,[19] and later came to connect "the problem of flesh and the end of metaphysics."[20]

In the first text I just evoked, Franck undertakes to think of the notion of *Leib* in terms of "flesh [*chair*]," rather than according to the expression *"corps propre"* which is the standard French translation of the *Leib* notion in the phenomenological jargon. [21]

In the light of such developments, it is therefore peculiar that, in his writing titled *Corpus*, Jean-Luc Nancy quotes as an example of a "philosophy of the 'body proper' "[22] precisely the passage in which Merleau-Ponty points out that "what we are calling flesh [. . .] has no name in any philosophy."[23] That is, a passage whose radical intentions rather allude to the *insufficiency* of a "philosophy of the 'body proper.' " On the other hand, this peculiar matching did not go unnoticed to Jacques Derrida in his *On Touching—Jean-Luc Nancy.*[24] Here he declares that, in the way Nancy mentions it, Merleau-Ponty's sentence is kept "at arm's length"[25] rather than being actually quoted. However, immediately afterward, Derrida interprets Nancy's gesture as an implicit "denunciation"[26] of that very sentence's content.

In any case, through Nancy's, Derrida's, and—as we shall see further on—Michel Henry's reflections, the notion of "flesh" now appears to have come back forcefully in the core of the philosophical debate, beyond the limits of the Merleau-Pontian, French, and phenomenological intellectual environment.

Here I would like to question some of this debate's issues and move toward some of its political as well as aesthetic implications, in order to make them explicit and to discuss them. Such implications will only appear in the second place. This, however, shall not be misinterpreted by deducting that we are here sharing the traditional metaphysical reasoning according to which to a certain philosophy respond *its own* politics and *its own* aesthetics, as if the former legitimated the latter, as if they were its consequences. Moving toward such implications of a philosophical proposition rather means moving toward the very core of this proposition as well as moving toward philosophy as such. Namely, the very core that is one and the same with the ontology manifesting itself as "practice, and experience, of the being-in-common,"[27] which we are urged to question precisely *because of this.*

As the previous reference hinted, in *Corpus*, Jean-Luc Nancy had criticized the notion of "body proper," pointing out that it seems inevitably to refer to "Property itself, Being-to-itself [*l'Être à soi*] embodied. But," countered Nancy, "instantly, always, the body on display is foreign, a monster that can't be swallowed."[28] Moreover, as Didier Franck had wondered even earlier: Is it really certain that the limits of my flesh are the ones of the body proper?[29] Shall we not push the flesh as far as "everything that we perceive, [extending it] unto the stars,"[30] to use a Bergsonian expression also quoted by Merleau-Ponty?

Precisely in the light of these questions, in *On Touching—Jean-Luc Nancy*, Derrida tends to accept the proposal advanced by Didier Franck to "substitute 'flesh' for 'body proper' [. . .]," and to do so, as Derrida points out, "despite the risk of some unreadable connotations that 'flesh' may risk importing [. . .] where the question of the 'Christian body' keeps reopening."[31]

Still, in the case of the term *leibhaftig*—often used by both Husserl and Heidegger to express a certain nonrepresentative and nonsubstitutive relationship to the relevant thing—Derrida tries to reject every attempt to burden the reference to the "flesh" with whatever meaning that goes beyond a "vaguely and conventionally metaphorical"[32] use. For his part, Merleau-Ponty expressly wrote that "[w]hen we say that the perceived thing is grasped 'in person' or 'in the flesh' (*leibhaft*), this is to be taken literally: the flesh of what is perceived [. . .] reflect[s] my own incarnation and [is] its counterpart."[33]

Derrida's perspective thus rejects the tendency of "bestowing a flesh upon 'things,' 'essences,' and modes of experience that are fleshless (without *Leib*) by essence, and without self-relation or self-contact."[34] In other words, in his opinion, only self-affection is evidence of the *Leiblichkeit*. By taking up again the terms of Merleau-Ponty's commentary on "Foundational

Investigations of the Phenomenological Origin of the Spatiality of Nature," we should then talk about a "kinship" that from the being of my body (*Leib*) "extends to others, who appear to me as 'other bodies,' to animals whom I understand as variants of my embodiment,"[35] *without*, however, going as far as the "terrestrial bodies," whose example par excellence is the stone.

Henry, Flesh, and Mud

Several points of convergence can be found between the main background notions of Derrida's writing and the premises of the work published by Michel Henry a few months later and titled *Incarnation. Une philosophie de la chair*,[36] namely, an explicitly Christian-inspired "philosophy of the flesh."

In fact, since the very first page of the "Introduction," Henry announces his intention of excluding from his inquiry "all living beings other than men," on account of the "methodological choice [. . .] of speaking of what we know rather than of what we don't know."[37] Nonetheless, in the following page he points out that self-affection is the distinctive feature of the "flesh": "We shall fix from the very beginning, through an appropriate terminology, this difference between the two bodies we have just distinguished—that is, on the one hand, our body experiencing itself feeling what surrounds it, and, on the other hand, an inert body of the universe, be it a stone on the road or the physical microparticles it is supposedly made of. We will call *flesh* the first, reserving the use of the term *body* for the latter."[38]

Such a layout leads us to express the aforementioned formulation as an opposition: "being defined by everything a mere body lacks, the flesh would not be able to blend with it. In fact, we might say that the flesh is rather the exact contrary. Flesh and body are opposed as feeling and not feeling—i.e., on the one hand, what gets enjoyment from itself; on the other hand, the blind, opaque, inert matter."[39]

According to Henry, an "abyss"[40] opens wide between the two terms. Concerning the first one, we would benefit from an "absolute and uninterrupted [although nonconceptual] knowledge." "Concerning the second one, we would be in "complete ignorance."[41] Provided that this is Henry's layout, it is my opinion that it should be brought back to his intention of inserting the "flesh elucidation"[42] theme in that of "Incarnation in a Christian sense."[43] Or, even better—as he specifies further—in St. John's sense.[44] In fact, Henry explains that in *De carne Christi* Tertullian links the flesh that Christ and mankind have in common to the mud that God, according to the Bible (Genesis 2:7), used to shape mankind itself.[45] Thus are outlined, in a clearly mythical form, the conditions of possibility of the "kinship" between our flesh, the earth's being, and the being of other bodies.[46] However, Henry rejects that link between flesh and mud. As he writes, *"in the earth's mud, there is no flesh, only bodies."*[47] Henry rather turns to the link announced in the fourteenth verse of John's Gospel's "Prologue": "And the Word was made flesh [καὶ ὁ λόγος σὰρξ ἐγένετο]." According to Henry, not from mud, but from the Word comes the flesh uniting mankind to the Christ. Therefore, as we have already noticed, the flesh proves in his opinion to be incomparable both with "inert bodies of material nature"[48] and with "living beings other than men."

In order to compare the layouts examined so far and to clarify their relevant implications, we shall consider as particularly significant certain consequences that, for Henry, are produced by this connection between flesh and Word. Namely, the flesh coming from the Word can neither be divided nor torn, with the exception of *"experienced impressions, none of which has been found yet in searching the earth's soil."*[49] Such flesh, then, *"is always somebody's flesh, mine for instance; so that it carries in itself an 'ego.'"*[50] If the Gospel of John's "Prologue" characterizes the Word as "the Word of Life," then, according to Henry, Life cannot be identified with "the blind and impersonal modern thought—be it Schopenhauer's will to live or Freud's drive."[51] This is why, in his opinion, phenomenology should undergo a "reversal" of the presuppositions rooting it in that "Greek" way of thinking that remains incompatible with John's announcement, and having shaped it so far as a "phenomenology of the world or of Being." Then it could become the science of a revelation of Life in its absoluteness, of which the flesh and the Word are ways of expression.[52] Henry's book aims precisely at this project.

Nancy, Flesh, and Stone

Contrary to what Merleau-Ponty stated in his commentary to "Foundational Investigations of the Phenomenological Origin of the Spatiality of Nature," neither Derrida nor Henry maintain that the stone "flies." Strictly considering the universe of authors so far taken into account, it can be useful to recall a remark Nancy makes in one of his writings explicitly evoking *Corpus*. It is a remark on the famous Heideggerian affirmation according to which "the stone is worldless,"[53] since its "touching" the earth is in no way similar to that of the lizard touching the stone, and even less to that of our hand resting on another person's head.[54] Nancy observes that "Heidegger's 'stone' is still merely abstract,"[55] since concretely, by its touching earth, "[t]here is difference of places—that is to say, place—dis-location, without appropriation of the place by another. There is not 'subject' and 'object,' but, rather, there are sites and places, distances [*écarts*]: a possible world that is already a world."[56] What Nancy specifies further seems precisely to answer the question concerning the limits of our *Leib*'s kinship (a question coinciding with that, otherwise formulated above, of the conditions of possibility of the experience communication). Indeed, Nancy writes as follows: "Am I in the process of suggesting that something of 'comprehension' can be attributed to the stone itself? One need not fear that I am proposing here an animism or a panpsychism. It is not a matter of endowing the stone with an interiority. But the very compactness of its impenetrable hardness (impenetrable to itself) can be defined (or can define itself, precisely) only through the distance [*écart*], the distinction of its being this here [. . .]. Thus, no animism—indeed, quite the contrary. Instead, a 'quantum philosophy of nature' [. . .] remains to be thought. Corpus: all bodies, each outside the others, make up the inorganic body of sense."[57]

Merleau-Ponty seems to move in a similar direction, when he states that the contact between my hands and that between my hand and a thing prove to be *akin* on account of a reversibility remaining—as I already recalled—"always imminent and never actually realized," thus celebrating the differentiating (and as such signifying) power of the distance [*écart*]. Actually, I would like to at least hint at the fact that Merleau-Ponty claims the carnal rooting of science when questioning precisely the problem of "the philosophical significance of quantum mechanics."[58]

Therefore, Merleau-Ponty's and Nancy's thinking directions seem to converge in recognizing the participation of the stone in the same world to which we belong ourselves.[59] With clear critical reference to Merleau-Ponty's later thought, Derrida, for his part, rejects—due to the previously argued reasons—the hypothesis of a "globalization [*mondialisation*] of flesh."[60] Hence, his remarks urge us to question whether it is possible to maintain phenomenology's programmatic intention to reinstate appearing into Being, isolating it at once from its unwanted implications (such as they are, at least, for Derrida).

Merleau-Ponty, Freudianism, and Flesh

As an example, it makes sense to question the position of the precisely "ontological" interpretation of psychoanalysis proposed by Merleau-Ponty's later thought. From his standpoint, such an interpretation redeems psychoanalysis at once from the scientist causalism whose presence Merleau-Ponty often notices in the Freudian language, as well as, on the one hand, from the "anthropological"[61] limits assigned to psychoanalysis, and, on the other hand, from the idea of stratification,[62] which we have seen Merleau-Ponty criticize with reference to Husserl.

The urge not to make "an existential psychoanalysis, but an *onto-logical* psychoanalysis"[63] is explicitly affirmed in a working note of the *Visible and the Invisible*, whose title significantly associates the conceptual "body and flesh" couple with the notion of "eros" in order to make the "Philosophy of Freudianism"[64] emerge from their connection.

This working note begins by reasserting Merleau-Ponty's criticism of the causalistic interpretation of what Freud calls "the relationship between on the one hand children's impressions [*Kindheitseindrücken*] and the artist's destiny, and on the other his works as reactions to these stimuli."[65] Here is the text of Merleau-Ponty's passage: "Superficial interpretation of Freudianism: he is a sculptor because he is anal, because the feces are already clay, molding, etc. But the feces are not the *cause*: if they were, everybody would be sculptors. The feces give rise to a character (*Abscheu*) only if the subject lives them in such a way as to find in them a dimension of being."[66]

With regard to this last expression, which is typical of Merleau-Ponty's later thought, it is worth recalling that the term *dimension* has to be understood as an *element* in the pre-Socratic sense I mentioned before, and in Bachelard's sense, as Merleau-Ponty himself specifies.[67] Such an element will never cease to define the relationship of that "subject"[68] with Being, resignifying itself from time to time in concurrence with the developments of that very relationship.

Going back to the examined working note, it carries on as follows: "In other words, to be anal *explains* nothing: for, to be so, it is necessary to have the ontological capacity (capacity to take a being as representative of Being)."[69] What Merleau-Ponty calls "ontological capacity" consists all in all in the possibility to invest any being (in a further working note the example of the sea is introduced) "as 'element,' and not as individual thing,"[70] through which the "openness to Being"[71] takes place.

It is clear, however, that such a capacity is denied whenever one advocates, as Derrida does, that our kinship with other bodies is confined to the ones for whom self-affection is possible. Still, the Eros that is appropriately summoned up in the title of Merleau-Ponty's working note, certainly can be invested in *things*, as testified by the phenomenon of fetishism, as well as in those ideals—namely, the essences, to which Derrida denies any carnal consistence, as much as he denied it to things—whose elaboration process is, according to Freud, similar to that of fetishes. Indeed, "[i]n this connection we can understand how it is that the objects to which men give most preference, their ideals, proceed from the same perceptions and experiences as the objects which they most abhor, and that they were originally only distinguished from one another through slight modifications. Indeed, as we found in tracing the origin of the fetish, it is possible for the original instinctual representative to be split in two, one part undergoing repression, while the remainder, precisely on the account of this intimate connection, undergoes idealization."[72]

Flesh, Stone, and Politics

However, does acknowledging a kinship between things and our *Leib* not imply (or, at least, risk to imply) an annihilation of their nature of *Körper*? A line of answer to that question may be found outlined once again in "Foundational Investigations of the Phenomenological Origin of the Spatiality of Nature." Here Husserl considers the hypothesis that "I and [. . .] we were able to fly and have two earths as soil-bodies, being able to arrive at the one from the other by flight. Precisely in this way the one would become body for the other, which would work as soil. But what do two earths mean? Two pieces of one earth with one humanity. Together, they would become one soil and, at the same time, each would be a body for the other."[73] Hence, the inclusion of the *Körper* in the *Leib* horizon does not erase its *Körperlichkeit*. Rather, it inaugurates the reversibility—"always imminent and never actually realized"—between its being *Körper* and its being *Leib*.

If one looks deeper, similar worries to those underpinning the question above have been recurrently raised as objections to the later thought of Merleau-Ponty. Sartre already complained that "Merleau-Ponty developed the habit of following each No until he saw it transformed into Yes, and each Yes until it changed it into No. He became so skillful at this *jeu de furet* that he virtually developed it into a method."[74]

Jean-François Lyotard later revived this perplexity, noticing Merleau-

Ponty's tendency to ignore "dissonances" in favor of "consonances."[75] The political implications of these remarks are evident. Sartre himself evoked them when writing that in Merleau-Ponty "contradictory truths never fight one another. There is no danger of their blocking movement or provoking an explosion. Moreover, are they, strictly speaking, contradictory?"[76] Merleau-Ponty's later thought would thus dilute contradictions so as to make them unthinkable as such, and therefore would open up to basically consolatory outcomes.

From a different standpoint, the clearly political necessity of not ignoring "dissonances" in favor of "consonances" seems at work in the book where Jean-Luc Nancy reflects on his own experience of undergoing a heart transplant. In explaining the basic underpinning of the book, he claims as follows: "I was asked for an article on the theme 'the stranger's coming.' I did not quite know what to do. I had just one idea: *to insist on the extraneousness of the stranger (instead of reabsorbing everything in the proximity, brotherhood, etc.).*"[77]

With regard to the problems analyzed so far, it is particularly meaningful that a text so explicitly prompted by such a necessity, comes to draw the conclusion that "the intruder is nothing but myself and man himself. None other than the same, never done with being altered, at once sharpened and exhausted, denuded and overequipped, an intruder in the world as well as in himself."[78]

What does emerge between that necessity and those outcomes? In a nearly intermediate position, Nancy describes in his text his own experience as a cardiac patient, which casts light on the inside-outside relationships—and even: the *intimate-extraneous* relationships—in terms that, referring to Merleau-Ponty, we could call *chiasmic*. "My heart became my stranger: stranger precisely because it was inside. *The strangeness could only come from outside because it surged up first on the inside.*"[79]

Precisely because of the emergence of this chiasm, Nancy's writing—prompted by the demand to emphasize the intruder's irremediable intrusiveness—seems to go as far as to announce that the intruder is *always already inside*, because "it is nobody else than me."

Could these outcomes be judged in their turn as consolatory? No, because although the stranger, being flesh of my own flesh, is as such my brother, my brother could indeed be Cain. *Actually, I may even be Cain myself.* As a condition of *all* these possibilities, as a condition of "a reversibility always imminent and never actually realized," the flesh founds *every* possible ethics and *every* possible politics. This means, on the one hand, that it does not found *a* particular ethic or *a* particular politic, and, on the other hand, that it cannot be considered as a "pre-ethical" or "pre-political" dimension, but that it rather constitutes the very horizon of our "being-in-common."[80]

Transposed to the terms of the question concerning the risk of an annihilation of the *Körper* into the *Leib*, these conclusions would not only point out that the stone is indeed within the horizon of the flesh, but also that we should be careful, for within the horizon of the flesh we might come across the stone. To state the absolute distinction between the flesh and the stone, between the stranger and the familiar, between the friend and the intruder, as if someone having exterminated his or her own family were not part of it, this would definitely be consolatory. It would in fact be consolatory to think of a reversibility without gaps (*écarts*), that could *realize itself* as a pacified con-fusion between the elements it relates. It would be just as consolatory to think of the distance (*écart*) as a fracture that, instead of *conjointly* opening the different—and divergent—possibilities of such elements, would set their absolute distinction and therefore their reciprocal *extrusion*. Within this last tendency, the orientation of those stating the irreducible specificity of the man's flesh as associated with incarnation (in the Christian sense of this term) is exposed to the risk of reproposing even for men the very position that founded, in the Western history, the modern strategies of both subjectivation and subjection.

Globalization, the "Virtual Field," and the Semantics of the Flesh

Roberto Esposito affirms something along the same lines as what I just outlined. In an original combination of Nancy and Merleau-Ponty,[81] he writes: "Philosophy cannot be but philosophy of relation, in relation, for relation. It is the point of resonance of the flesh of the world."[82] This is of course an orientation opposed to that of Derrida, and to his rejection of a "globalization [*mondialisation*] of flesh."

However, this expression does not only evoke the Merleau-Pontian theme claimed by Esposito. In fact, the French term *mondialisation* is indeed the one designating the current economic and cultural globalization process.

Which are the resonances produced by the combination of such a process and a thinking of the flesh? One, for instance, is that the conception of the flesh I defined above as *texture of differences* leads Merleau-Ponty, at the end of a working note significantly titled "Chiasm-Reversibility," to wonder: "What do I bring to the problem of the same and the other? This: that the same be the other than the other, and identify difference of difference."[83] The identity defining me, then, consists in perceiving myself as different from the differences constituting others. For instance, this means that I would perceive myself as *Italian* coming across the difference of a *French* person; while facing that of an American, I would rather perceive myself as *European*, suddenly bestowing that same identity on the French person as well, which will make him or her appear as similar to me, rather than different. Still, it is evident that this dynamic is not specific to the time of globalization following the fall of the Berlin Wall and characterized by the event of electronic trade. Indeed, in the same way that, thirty-five years ago the son of a Southern immigrant based in Northern Italy would feel Southern only when hearing certain Northern judgments on his father's fellow countrymen, and he would feel Northern, and utterly so, only when visiting his father's family.

Such examples point out that, if considered in the terms suggested by this conception of flesh, identity is never established once and for all, but always defined anew by the *encounter* with the other's difference. Identity consequently reveals itself to be the *virtual center* never ceasing to define itself through one's always renewed differentiation movement with relation to the other's differences. Thus, the vertiginous acceleration imposed on certain transformations by the *current forms* of globalization[84] emphasizes the way in which the flesh is constitutively "global [*mondiale*]."

This direction of thought is reintroduced and specified by Roberto Esposito within a "Dialogue on the Philosophy to Come" with Jean-Luc Nancy.[85] Despite what we read above concerning his critics against the notion of "body proper," in this dialogue Nancy affirms his preference for a thinking of the body rather than of the flesh, which he qualifies as "a word of depth while body is a light word."[86] Toward Nancy's reasons, Esposito objects with some reflections that it would be useful to mention, at least in their main articulations:

> Rather, it seems to me that the principle of alteration or contamination evokes instead the semantics of "flesh" understood exactly as the opening of the body, the body's expropriation, its "common" being. [. . .] Flesh refers to the outside as body does to the inside: it is the point and the margin in which the body is no longer just a body but is also its reverse and its base sundered, as Merleau-Ponty had intuited. [. . .] I believe that the first task of a philosophy to come is above all that of

replacing terms like "earth," "body," and 'immunity,' with terms like "world," "flesh," and "community."[87]

In his turn, Pietro Montani followed up this line of thought—this semantics of "flesh"—by developing it in an original way within the field of aesthetics and pointing out that such a line of thought brings along "important repercussions as far as images are concerned."[88] Such repercussions evidently also conjugate with the technological mutations at work in this field.

No wonder that, from such a perspective, the semantics of the Merleau-Pontian flesh inspires a volume "entitled *Aesthetics of the Virtual* because it deals with bodies that are images, with the interactions between our body—weighted down but at the same time lightened by inorganic prostheses—and those images."[89] In fact, the volume's author, Roberto Diodato, explains that, in his view, the notion of "flesh of the world" is "a good descriptor of the virtual field"[90] insofar as this very "virtual field, whose objects are modalities of relation, is itself a structure of the correlation or relational texture of bodies understood as events of reversibility."[91]

Whether we are taking into account the digital revolution or globalization, what the semantics of the Merleau-Pontian flesh helps us to think and name is always such a texture of relations between differences. And indeed, it can also prevent us from separating aesthetics from politics.

Chapter Two

It Takes a Long Time to Become Wild

Gauguin According to Merleau-Ponty,
Merleau-Ponty According to Gauguin

What Flesh? Derrida Against Merleau-Ponty

In the beginning of what was to remain the last chapter of the unfinished work *The Prose of the World*,[1] Merleau-Ponty reminds us that "[n]owadays we encourage every form of illusive and allusive expression, especially pictorial expression, and in particular the art of the 'primitives,' the drawings of the children and madmen. [. . .] But [. . .] the resort to brute expression has not occurred in opposition to the art of the museums."[2]

Just before this chapter suddenly comes to a halt, Merleau-Ponty goes back to the so-characterized pictorial expression, by writing that "[t]he objects in a modern painting 'bleed,' their substance spreads under our eyes, they directly question our gaze, and they test the pact of coexistence that we have made with the world by means of our whole body."[3]

In the so-specified sense, we can thus relate to modern painting as a whole what, in *The Visible and the Invisible*, Merleau-Ponty was to remark on by referring in particular to Paul Klee's work: namely, a certain trend he defined as "painting without identifiable things, without the *skin* of things, but giving their *flesh*."[4]

In short, to Merleau-Ponty, in modern painting the flesh is *at stake*— both the flesh of things (a better term than *objects*, whose etymology would suggest their *being absolutely in front of us*), and the flesh constituting each living creature's way of *inhabiting the world.*

Besides, we know that in *On Touching—Jean-Luc Nancy*, Jacques Derrida blames Merleau-Ponty for the multiple aspects of a supposed fundamental infidelity to Husserl.[5] Derrida, on the one hand, affirms that Husserl would have never shared the Merleau-Pontian notion of "flesh of the world,"[6] and, on the other hand, judges as dangerous "the more or less systematic translation of *Leib* by 'flesh,'" since to him it risks importing some "unerasable connotations," "where the question of the 'Christian body' keeps reopening. To be sure, not everything in the word 'flesh' comes down to Christian semantics; asserting such a thing would be absurd or imprudent. However, it would be equally imprudent to ignore the filing and scraping action of this semantics, even where the ones using this word may be anything except 'Christians' and would not for a single moment dream of putting their discourse about flesh at the service of a Christian cause intentionally."[7]

It is precisely in the context of this discussion, whose accents resonate in such a peculiarly philosophical way, that I mean to appeal to the artistic witness of Paul Gauguin.

Wild Being, Being Wild

As we have seen, the art of the "primitives" is accounted by Merleau-Ponty among the forms of expressions that were privileged by modern painting. Also, it is well known that, precisely in this sense, Gauguin is considered to be "the *primitif* of modernist primitivism, its original, seminal figure."[8] Apparently, Merleau-Ponty never focused his philosophical reflection on Gauguin's pictorial research. Still, their mutual attention to the "wild Being"—meant as an actual dimension which "is asked to create culture anew,"[9] and Western culture in the first place—seems to make their purposes spontaneously convergent.

I thus mean to approach the painting and pictorial poetics that Gauguin developed in Polynesia according to the notions of "flesh" and "wild Being" elaborated by Merleau-Ponty. From such a perspective, my aim is, on the one hand, to verify whether the aforementioned theoretical notions can help us better understand the sense of Gauguin's pictorial attempt, and on the other hand, to evaluate, by means of their confrontation with Gauguin's painting, the reach of these very notions, especially in relation to Derrida's judgments, which I just recalled.

As we know, Merleau-Ponty conceives the originating as being in perpetual explosion. In this sense, he remarks that "it is not a question of becoming wild anew."[10] Indeed not, if this means performing a regression that would allow us eventually to stick to a positive layer of experience preceding all cultures and hence characterizing itself as intact; namely, a layer we would later wish to *expose* in a mimetic way.

In a working note of *The Visible and the Invisible*, Merleau-Ponty rather identifies the wild Being with the "perceived world,"[11] whose relation with painting he had then just described as follows: "The 'amorphous' perceptual world that I spoke of in relation to painting—perpetual resources for the remaking of painting—which contains no mode of expression and which nonetheless calls them forth and requires all of them and which arouses again with each painter a new effort of expression [. . .] this perceptual world is [. . .] more than all painting, than all speech, than every 'attitude,' and [. . .] appears as containing everything that will be said, and *yet leaving us to create it.*"[12]

Similarly, the *wildness* to which Gauguin tends seems to consist, in the first place, in a relation to nature that is not *imitative*, but *creative*, capable of meeting its "mysterious infinites," its "imaginative power," to the never-ending variation of its "productions," as Gauguin himself writes apropos of Redon in 1889.[13] Also, in its vibrations, such a relation to nature should be capable of intercepting "what is most general and therefore most undefinable in nature: its inner power," as he reaffirms nearly ten years later.[14] This appears several times in his *Writings of a Savage*, where Gauguin rejects precisely the "servile imitation of nature,"[15] claiming that one should rather observe how nature itself is "*artist*,"[16] and observe it, as he specifies, in a "personal" way, with the aim of taking a personal "science"[17] out of it. In short, as synthesized in the "Notebook for Aline," "an artist [. . .] (if he really wants to produce a divine creative work), must not copy nature but take the natural elements and create a new element."[18]

For Gauguin as well as for Merleau-Ponty, the expression of the wild Being thus consists in a "creative repetition [*reprise créatrice*]"[19] of this *erste Natur* that the philosopher significantly defines as a "barbaric Principle,"[20] describing it as "the most ancient element, 'an abyss of the past' which always remains present in us and in all things."[21]

For both Gauguin and Merleau-Ponty, the expression of the wild Being thus exists by a gesture that is at once *archeological* and *teleological*. In this sense, Gauguin envisages translating "a truth by a lie."[22] And it is the *sign* (not the *model*)[23] of this very gesture, of this "truthfulness of falsehood,"[24] that he looks for in several artistic experiences, which are mostly—although not exclusively—"primitive."

This is where he gets the tendency for an artistic "eclecticism"[25]—"Daumier meets Giotto in Japan,"[26] as it has been written—namely, that lack of coherence with regard to the primitivism he has often been associated with.[27] Such an eclecticism, as Merleau-Ponty put it, would not allow opposition of "brute expression [. . .] to the art of the museums." What follows, in a more general way, is Gauguin's inclination to "cultural syncretism"[28] that, "in the spirit of theosophy,"[29] leads him step by step to the conception of a fundamental unity of all religions underpinning many of his Tahitian paintings, which is suggested in the manuscript titled *L'esprit moderne et le catholicisme*.[30]

Evidently, professing this cultural syncretism and this spirit of theosophy is not enough "to avoid professing oneself Christian," as Benedetto Croce would have said. Still, in Gauguin's works, the flesh of the Tahitian women does not look very much like a Christian flesh, despite the Christian references the painter sometimes introduces in his pictures. Such references can rather be led back to the syncretic inclination we just recalled. Indeed, I would rather say that, precisely in the name of such an inclination, Gauguin seems to engage his pictorial path in a most original "*deconstruction of the Christian 'flesh,'*" as Derrida writes about Nancy.[31]

Gauguin and the Deconstruction of the Christian "Flesh"

It seems to me that it is precisely by moving in this direction that Gauguin makes a characteristic detour through stone or wood. In fact, in his works, the Tahitian women's bodies—even those that are drawn or painted—are sculptural bodies. "Sculptural form"[31] is indeed the expression Gauguin himself uses in the manuscript of *Noa Noa*, in order to designate the carnal kinship he believes he sees between the body of King Pomare's woman and a temple's pediment. Still, in *Noa Noa*—apropos of the woman he is about to paint in *Vahine no te tiare* (1891)—he writes that her mouth appears to him as if it had been "modelled by a sculptor."[33] Similarly, he observes that Tehamana's body reminds him of "a perfect idol."[34] Also, in a letter to André Fontainas written in March 1899, he resorts to the term "statuesque" to qualify the "rigidity" of some "animal shapes," significantly linking them to something "indescribably antique, august, and religious in the rhythm of their gesture, in their singular immobility."[35] But the fact of pursuing the flesh in its kinship with stone or wood so as to get back to its primitive sacrality becomes an actual and explicit declaration of intention where, in announcing in "Miscellaneous Things" "the painting I want to do"—which is, as we know, a nonexecuted painting—Gauguin explains that "The main figure will be a woman turning into a statue, still remaining alive yet becoming an idol."[36]

Indeed, here Gauguin aims at pursuing the carnal up to the *impossible con-fusion* with the sculptural, with the objective of winning back its primitive sacrality, by showing the cobelonging of what is animate and what is inanimate. It is in this sense that he seems to aspire to "deconstruct" what Derrida defined as the Christian "unerasable connotations" of the flesh, and to do so by a detour through stone or wood, a detour such as to give back to this flesh a sacrality that—let us pay attention to this—is not only wild, but at the same time also Greek. Indeed, Gauguin's intolerance towards Greek art, meant as an *obliged model*, is known as much as his tendency to turn it into one of his many inspiration sources, as in the case of *Eh quoi, tu es jalouse?* (1892), where "the central figure is based on the statue of Dionysos, a picture of which Gauguin has taken to Tahiti."[37]

Actually, the presence of Greek art amid Gauguin's sources of inspiration confirms his eclecticism, which, in its turn, seems to obey the fundamental intentions of that cultural syncretism by which he planned to put in light the secret connection he sensed between the Tahitian culture and "other, grander cultures."[38] What evidently corresponds to this connection is a particular attention to polytheist religions, which the Greek and the Tahitian both are. It is just as evident that such an attention is one and the same with Gauguin's aforementioned attempt to draw from a primitive sacrality, which—as he explains in "The Catholic Church and Modern Times"[39]—does not turn God into an invention to solve the "unfathomable mystery."[40] It is not less evident either that such an attention toward polytheist religions and such an attempt to draw from a primitive sacrality are in their turn one and the same with the engagement to attain the "deconstruction of the Christian 'flesh'" that is proper to him. In fact, as Jean-Luc Nancy reminds us, in Christian monotheism the man-God is the one who, on the one hand, shows himself and, on the other hand, withdraws. On the contrary, the Tahitian gods, just like the Greek, have the "essential propriety" Nancy indicates in polytheism: that is, "[t]he plurality of the gods constitutes their visibility, whether potential or actual, as well as their presence. The art of polytheism provides a vision of the gods, while that of monotheism recalls the invisibility of God withdrawn into His unity."[41]

In sum, Nancy highlights the different *visibility* of the polytheist gods, on the one hand, and, on the other hand, of the "present/hidden and presenting himself as hidden"[42] Christian god, as well as of the monotheist religions in general. On this issue, it is important to recall once more that it is indeed by "visibility" that Merleau-Ponty characterizes what we heard him call "flesh," explaining that such visibility is not restricted to the mere ensemble of visibles composing what Merleau-Ponty calls "primary visibility,"[43] but also embraces the lines of force and the dimensions that the visibles suggest, thus generating a "second visibility"[44] entangling and surrounding the first.

Veiled and Opaque: On Visibility in Painting

Hence, what opens up within the questioning that concerns us here is the theme of the visibility of flesh in painting, namely, the theme that is traditionally indicated precisely by the French term *incarnat* [complexion]. Regarding this issue, it seems to me it is first of all important to point out—as Georges Didi-Huberman did—that, although the term incarnat [complexion] is generally used to designate the pictorial representation of the skin [*peau*], it is paradoxically not composed after this latter term, but after the French word *chair* [flesh].[45] Moreover, what I have been writing so far imposes the question of whether complexion [*incarnat*] in Christian painting has a particular characteristic. It is evident that the answer to such a question cannot but refer to a trend. Jean-Luc Nancy's characterization of Christian monotheism, which I just recalled, can help us find that answer. Indeed, if "the Christian god 'properly' (religiously) understood" is "present/concealed and presentifying himself concealed," then I believe it is possible to affirm first of all that, in Christian painting, complexion [*incarnat*] tends to present a withdrawing god. More precisely, it presents the god's "retreat" [*retrait*].[46] And I shall add that, precisely in his attempt to characterize Christian painting, Nancy, on the one hand, focuses his attention on the "exposure of the skin or the veil,"[47] and, on the other hand, reminds us that, in the passage from the visibility of Greek polytheism to that of Christian monotheism, Plotinus occupies a fundamental position. Indeed, it is well known that Plotinus celebrates the sensible only insofar as it does not cease to refer to a supersensible otherness, thus opening up for men—as Erwin Panofsky significantly points out—"the prospect of the world of Ideas but at the same time veiling the view."[48] Such a conception of the "veil" of the sensible is precisely what seems to be transposed to complexion [*incarnat*] in Christian painting. Indeed, rather than that "compact particle which stops exploration" defining "the flesh of the sensible" according to Merleau-Ponty,[49] here the skin [*peau*] is, on the contrary, a veil. In fact, it presents itself to our look as if it were illuminated by a divine principle whose source, at the same time, it conceals.

This layout thus allows us, by contrast, to better see at work the "deconstruction of the Christian 'flesh' " in which Gauguin's painting seems to be engaged. Indeed, by a detour through stone or wood, Gauguin's painting gives back to the skin the opacity that the Merleau-Pontian passage I just quoted also meant to evoke. An example may be Tehamana's body in *Manao Tupapau* (1892): by the opacity of its dark skin, it recalls—as through a passage from negative to positive—the utterly white and yet no less opaque skin of Manet's *Olympia*, which Gauguin admired so much.[50] In fact, if one looks deeper, to give back to skin such an opacity means to give back to skin its *unity with flesh*, thus denying the skin's status of mere "envelope" of bodies from which, precisely for this reason and as Merleau-Ponty has reminded us, most of modern painting tried to move away. On the other hand, to give back to the flesh its *unity with skin* means to release, in its turn, the flesh from the connotation of interiority that has produced its ambiguous spiritualization, by which it was considered as precariously inhabited by the "present/concealed and presentifying [it] self concealed" divine principle also named "soul." Eventually, to give back to the skin its opacity also means to give back to the flesh [*chair*] its consistency, so as to avoid reducing complexion [*incarnat*] to a veil which, in presenting a metaphysical light, cannot but present at once its retreat. On the contrary, Christian painting seems to *have constituted itself* of such a tendency, referring back to an eschatological *fall of the veil*, that is to say, eschatologically referring to the full visibility of that god who does not cease to withdraw "in His unity."

It is thanks to the detour through stone or wood that Gauguin, on the contrary, tries to reintroduce a sacrality of Nature understood as the wild Being to whom the animate and the inanimate belong and in whom they belong to each other, hence, understood as flesh of their shared visibility. Such visibility, being "primary" as well as "secondary," in no way refers to a metaphysical principle and does not promise any eschatological *fall of the veil*. Thus, by combining the teaching of polytheist religions with the Western sensibility to the "death of god,"[51] such visibility rather proclaims—as Nietzsche does in the "Preface for the Second Edition" of *The Gay Science* that Merleau-Ponty quotes in his last course—"we no longer believe that truth remains truth when the veils are withdrawn."[52]

This has to be better detailed. In Merleau-Ponty the fact of hierarchizing a "primary" and a "secondary" visibility of the visible itself—the "second" being that of its invisible halo—has only a heuristic value. Still, the very fact of this hierarchization seems to confess the visible's *civilized* characterization, against Gauguin's effort to re-create a "primitive" way of seeing, in which such a hierarchy cannot but appear problematic. Paintings like *La vision du sermon* (1888) and, once again, *Manao Tupapau* are clear examples of this consideration. Indeed, in these works, the magical-religious element—that is, the Breton peasants' hallucination as well as Tehamana's—is *present* on the canvas as being intentionally indistinct from the sensible itself.[53] In such works the copresence of real and imaginary is thus effectively *made visible*. And to show this copresence is to claim once more the *actuality* of the mythical-symbolic dimension—that is, the "wild Being"—nourishing primitive sacrality.

When one looks deeper, the cobelonging of animate and inanimate is given precisely within such a copresence of real and imaginary. In its turn, animism—that very animism which is duly recalled apropos of Tehamana's hallucination in *Manao Tupapau*[54]—also takes its roots in the cobelonging of animate and inanimate. And no less than animism, the notion of "flesh of the world" elaborated by Merleau-Ponty also seems to be rooted in the cobelonging of animate and inanimate. This way, it reveals itself to be something completely different from the "Christian figure" denounced by Derrida.

It is as animated by a similar search that the work of Gauguin, by its detour through stone or wood, has appeared to me to be as engaged in a so peculiar "deconstruction of the Christian 'flesh'" which is so characteristic. In fact, such a detour makes primitive connotations emerge even in the Christian references appearing in Gauguin's Polynesian paintings, thus achieving a search that can also be discovered in certain pictures he painted in Brittany, like *Calvaire breton* (1889), where the group of sacred characters evokes the figure of a totem. And it is not irrelevant to point out that totemism draws from the very wild Being to which the notion of "flesh of the world" itself seems to refer.[55]

Rather than Christian, this notion therefore presents itself as a *philosophical figure of primitivism* which—as Merleau-Ponty precisely suggested in the sentence I quoted at the beginning of this chapter—"nowadays we encourage." In particular, it constitutes a philosophical figure that is closer to Gauguin's primitivism rather than to the primitivism of the subsequent cubist generation, if it is true that the latter "would use primitivism as an arm against the very ambiguities and half-light mysteries Gauguin found so absorbing."[56]

For his part, Merleau-Ponty, in reaffirming the ambiguous copresence of real and imaginary, writes: "[o]ur waking relations with objects and others especially have an oneiric character as a matter of principle: objects and others are present to us in the way dreams are, the way myths are."[57]

As we have seen, the term *present* highlights in Nancy the different visibility of the polytheistic gods compared to the monotheistic religions' gods. In his way Gauguin seems to mean to specify that if "objects and others [. . .] are present to us in the way [. . .] myths are," this is because such a presence characterizes, firstly and mainly, our relation with the "unfathomable mystery" summarized in the three questions: *Where do we come from? What are we? Where are we going?*

Chapter Three

"Making Visible"

Merleau-Ponty and Paul Klee

The Visibility of the Invisible

Sichtbarmachen: "making visible." The essential terms of the famous sentence with which in 1920 Paul Klee opened his Creative Credo—"Art does not reproduce the visible; rather, it makes visible"[1]—are back six years later on the side of a drawing in which, in a vaguely anthropomorphic form, a door seems to appear, surrounded not by a wall, but by the opening of a starry sky. In fact, it has to be remarked that if art can make visible, it is because there is indeed a visibility of the invisible, which makes itself seen in the very genesis of the visible, that is, when the visible is "in its nascent state" ["*à l'état naissant*"]. As Merleau-Ponty recalled in the preparatory notes for one of his last courses, in the Creative Credo, Klee indeed wrote that "[t]he work of art, too, is above all a process of creation [*Auch das Kunstwerk ist in erster Linie Genesis*]."[2]

This is, hence, what the artist tries to figure out, as Klee explained four years later in a passage of the lecture significantly titled *On Modern Art*, which Merleau-Ponty had transcribed. According to Klee, "[t]he deeper [the artist] looks, the more readily he can extend his view from the present to the past, the more deeply he is impressed by the one essential image of creation itself, as Genesis."[3]

"[T]o grasp the sense of the world or of history in its nascent state" is also the objective Merleau-Ponty not only attributed to phenomenology and to himself, but that he would go so far as to identify with "the effort

31

of modern [or even contemporary] thought."[4] Within such an effort, he no doubt also included Klee's pictorial research, with which he gradually finds himself in a deep convergence.[5]

In 1959, many of Merleau-Ponty's preparatory notes for the 1958–59 course on "Philosophy Today" are consecrated precisely to Klee's research. This sizable ensemble of notes, to which I alluded above, is essentially based on the work of Grohmann,[6] and will lead Merleau-Ponty to the question "Why this insistence on Klee?,"[7] after having implicitly indicated that one of the answers can be found precisely in the theme, so dear to Klee, of the "genesis grasping," which we came across earlier.[8]

The previously echoed expression, that is, "visibility of the invisible," is proper to Merleau-Ponty. It appears in the last lecture theme he completed, at the end of his 1959–60 course at the Collège de France titled "Nature and Logos: The Human Body." Although he does not openly declare it, by such an expression Merleau-Ponty evidently meant to characterize his own philosophical research, which was then explicitly focused on the elaboration of a "new ontology."

As we have already seen in chapter 1, such a project found its roots and reasons in the "ontological rehabilitation of the sensible." To Merleau-Ponty, precisely this rehabilitation seemed to imply—according to the words of the above-quoted lecture theme—"a philosophy of the flesh as the visibility of the invisible."[9] That is to say, a philosophy which—in the light of such a rehabilitation—would get so far as to reconsider the very problem of the relationship between the sensible and the intelligible.

It is well known that Platonism had codified such a problem by means of an ontological devaluation of the sensible and by its opposition to the intelligible. In turn, such an opposition was linked to that of the two modes of vision: on the one hand, the carnal vision limited to the vision of the sensible world and, on the other hand, the intellectual vision contemplating the world of ideas.

Setting an "ontological rehabilitation of the sensible" thus, most evidently, means to move away from this heritage (and in fact means to "make visible" "creation itself as Genesis," as Klee envisaged) and to reconsider the relation between the sensible and the intelligible. At the very time of his death, Merleau-Ponty was working on this. It is indeed on this issue that the pages of his unfinished manuscript *The Visible and the Invisible* are interrupted.

The direction toward which such a work was to develop is indicated by the notes of the last courses Merleau-Ponty gave at the Collège de France. Indeed, they significantly explore the Concept of Nature, on the one hand, and "the possibility of philosophy today,"[10] on the other hand.

Concerning the theoretical question examined here, the preparatory notes for the course titled Cartesian Ontology and Today's Ontology are particularly illuminating. In fact, in these notes emerge precisely the development axes Merleau-Ponty was to follow in his new ontological articulation between the sensible and the intelligible. He considered such axes to be *at work* in contemporary ontology even though they had not yet been explicitly thematized from a philosophical point of view.

At the core of these development axes, a notion is finally thematized. Such a notion had insistently circulated before, even in the later texts, but always remained implicit (it is only formulated once in *Eye and Mind*).[11] However, it reveals itself to be *crucial* for "a philosophy of the flesh as the visibility of the invisible." Such is the notion designated by the term *voyance*, which indicates the gift of "double sight." In the attempt to fully understand its reach, I will link it (of course, after recalling—at least briefly—the general layout of the course in which it is situated) to the notes Merleau-Ponty consecrated two years earlier to Paul Klee's pictorial research.

The *Ut Pictura Poesis* Today

As I pointed out before, and as the title "Cartesian Ontology and Today's Ontology" itself points out, the aim of this 1960–61 course is that of searching—by contrast with the Cartesian ontology—a philosophical formulation of contemporary ontology. Such an ontology, according to Merleau-Ponty, has so far found its expression mainly in art, and particularly in literature.

The first step of his path thus consists in an exploration of the landscape of "contemporary ontology," which spontaneously and implicitly developed precisely in art and literature. "Especially in literature,"[12] as Merleau-Ponty specifies at a certain point, thus relativizing once and for all the role of exclusive reference some people had attributed to painting in the later phase of his philosophy.

The exploration of the artistic field is nonetheless focused on painting, and follows again the itinerary Merleau-Ponty had already traced over the previous summer when writing *Eye and Mind*. Klee's pictorial thought had a crucial role at the very core of this work.[13] In its turn, the exploration of the literary field aims at facing Proust's work as well as that of Valery, Claudel, and certain "recent literature"[14] figures, such as Saint-John Perse and Claude Simon.[15]

Although it had not been explicitly planned by this program, another literary reference will play a crucial role in the definition of the contemporary ontological landscape. This reference is Arthur Rimbaud's *Lettre du Voyant* [*Letter of the Seer*]. Merleau-Ponty gets there via a declaration of Max Ernst's, in which the artist assimilated the present task of the painter precisely to the one that Rimbaud's manifesto attributed to the poet. Here it is: "Just as the role of the poet since the famous *Lettre du voyant* consists in writing under the dictation of what is being thought, of what articulates itself in him, the painter's role is to circumscribe and project what is making itself seen within himself."[16]

From this perspective, *voyance* ends up naming that "new bond between the writer and the visible"[17] that Merleau-Ponty considers to be linked to the research he calls "modern" (though I have argued that it should be understood as contemporary), and which can rediscover the "Renaissance beyond Descartes."[18] As he explains, "[t]he moderns rediscover the Renaissance through the magical idea of visibility: it is the thing that makes itself seen (outside and inside), over there and here."[19] The nearly contemporary pages of the "Introduction" to *Signs* help clarify what this "magical idea of visibility" actually is: "the visible things and the visible world [. . .] are always behind what I see of them, as horizons, and what we call visibility is this very transcendence. No thing, no side of a thing, shows itself except by actively hiding the others, denouncing them in the act of concealing them."[20]

Merleau-Ponty thus considers that the literature of our epoch renews such a "magical idea of visibility" and is consequently characterized—according to Rimbaud's indication—as *voyance*. Indeed, Merleau-Ponty contends that "da Vinci vindicates the *voyance against* poetry,"[21] which, unlike painting, da Vinci himself considers to be "incapable of 'simultaneity,' "[22] and therefore incapable of teaching us—according to the meaningful definition of *Eye and Mind*—that "beings that are different, 'exterior,' foreign to one another, are yet absolutely *together*."[23] On the other hand, Merleau-Ponty remarks that "moderns make of poetry also a *voyance*."[24] Therefore, they show that poetry is indeed "capable of simultaneity."

Descartes had reduced vision to a kind of *thought* stimulated by images, as well as by signs and words. In contrast, Merleau-Ponty conjectures that the "unveiling of the 'voyance' in modern art—a *voyance* which is not the Cartesian thought—might have [an] analogue in the arts of *speech*."[25] As a consequence, he suggests that "[p]erhaps we should, instead of reducing vision to a reading of signs by thought, rediscover in speech, conversely, a transcendence of the same type that occurs in vision."[26] Indeed, he thinks Rimbaud decisively contributed precisely to this project. *Voyance*—which, in the mutual reference to perception and the imaginary, "renders present to us what is absent"[27]—therefore characterizes vision itself. Thus, vision is not what in Heideggerian terms would be called a *Vor-stellung*, that is "an operation of thought that would set up before the mind a picture or a representation of the world"[28]—namely an operation of *subjection* [*assujettissement*]. Seeing should instead be regarded as "seconding" ["*seconder*"]—a verb expressing the indistinguishability of activity and passivity—the *self-showing* of the sensible universe, within which we find ourselves and through which runs the power of analogy.[29] Such a power is the same one echoed in Baudelaire's *Correspondences*, a power in virtue of which the body and the things recall each other, by binding new relationships, inventing new lines of force, and vanishing lines: in short, by sketching a "logos of the aesthetic world."[30] Such is the Husserlian expression often recalled by Merleau-Ponty, implicating a radical reconsideration of the sensible-intelligible relation.

The characterization of seeing as a *seconding from within the visible* is in a peculiar consonance with the artist's "*gegenständliche Jawort*," which Klee echoes in his lecture delivered on the occasion of an exhibition at the Jena Kunstverein in 1924, and which Merleau-Ponty later quotes.[31] In my opinion, a contribution to such a characterization can also be found in the most effective expression chosen by Paul Claudel to title a book that never ceased to catch Merleau-Ponty's attention. Indeed, it is not by chance that this very expression is echoed in the pages that are in question here. Such an expression, which has been catching the attention of French phenomenological aesthetics in general, is *The Eye Listens*.[32] It is a formulation synesthetically refusing all analytic separation between the sensory fields, particularly between the supposed activity of seeing and the supposed passivity of listening.[33]

By this characterization of seeing, *voyance* helps specify the "mutation in the relationship between humanity and Being" that in *Eye and Mind* Merleau-Ponty confesses to feeling "when he holds up a universe of classical thought contrasting it en bloc with the explorations of modern painting."[34] In a working note for the *Visible and the Invisible*, he finds this same mutation manifest in "atonal music," which is assimilated to "painting without identifiable things, without the *skin* of things, but giving their *flesh*."[35] In other words, as specified in the course notes on Paul Klee, it is assimilated to a kind of painting that is "different from appearances [. . .] [s]ince it gives what nature means to say and yet does not say: the 'generating principle' which makes the things and the world be."[36]

In fact, the mutation felt by Merleau-Ponty consists in a *carnal* configuration of the relationship between humans and Being. This mutation is obviously not expressible in the language of consciousness, of representation, of the modern frontality of subject and object. This is why Merleau-Ponty judges contemporary literature as linking, with the visible, that "new bond" that might be configurable as *voyance*.

Hence, after examining the conception of language that Descartes expressed in the letter addressed to Mersenne on November 20, 1629, with regard to the idea of a universal language,[37] and after seeing in this conception "the equivalent of the theory of perspective,"[38] Merleau-Ponty turns to the contrasting contemporary conception of language, which, according to him, characterizes language "not as an instrument in which thought would be as the pilot in his boat—but as some sort of substantial union of thought and language—Language not governed, but endowed of its own efficacy."[39]

The *Lettre du voyant* becomes an emblem of this contemporary conception, since there the autonomy of language is pushed so far as to proclaim the becoming *voyance* of poetry. This is why Merleau-Ponty considers Rimbaud to be "a fundamental milestone within a development of literature which began before and continues after him."[40] Echoing that "mutation in the relationship between humanity and Being" that *Eye and Mind* sees expressed by painting, Merleau-Ponty writes that "it might be the case of a change of the relationship with the Being in the writer starting from Romanticism."[41] As we have already seen, the change he has in mind is a change of the relationship between the visibility of Being and the speech of the writer. This way, such a speech—instead of aiming at designating meanings[42]—mixes with things and, just as, for Rimbaud, "the wood [. . .] finds itself a violin," becomes a sensible emblem of the sensible itself.[43]

As we have seen, Merleau-Ponty remarks on a contemporary exigency of rediscovering in speech the "transcendence of the same type that occurs in vision," which he recognizes in Rimbaud's poetics of *voyance*. This transcendence of *voyance* is not a "second sight" directed to the intelligible, but rather a vision that sees the invisible in the visible and thus allows us to find, within the very fabric of music or of literary speech, as well as within the veil of the visible, the invisible of the idea that shines through. Christine Buci-Glucksmann wrote that "Visioning [*Voyance*]—by which things absent become present to us—defines simultaneously *the place of art and the access to Being*, the simultaneous appearance of an aesthetics and an 'ontology.'"[44] In the light of this observation, and considering what we have elaborated so far, we can point out that this *double appearance is* also *accompanied by that of a gnoseology*, since *voyance* is also defining "a *totally virtual Wesensschau* and, at the same time, *always already working* in the intuition (or in the vision, or, more generally, in the apprehension) of this or that phenomenon."[45]

In short, *voyance*, which in the being [*étant*] sees its Being [*Être*] appear, ends up emerging as the *Wesensschau* (the vision of essences) operated by a thinking that is not an absolute contemplating (*kosmotheoréin*), but is indissociable from the sensible vision: precisely, then, a *carnal Wesensschau*.[46] Therefore it linked to the carnal ideality I hinted at in chapter 1 of this book. In the following chapters we will examine it more closely by the name of "sensible idea."

Making Philosophy in a Baroque World

The "mutation in the relationship between humanity and Being" that Merleau-Ponty traces in the bond that, in our epoch, both the writer and the painter tie up with the visible, also requires an adequate philosophical expression. This, in turn, requires us to reconsider the very idea of philosophy. In the light of what his course notes indicate, Merleau-Ponty evidently does not suggest abdicating it, but rather reconsidering it by taking advantage of the experiences by virtue of which modern art and literature—prior to philosophy—were able to give a full expression to that mutation.

In a working note of *The Visible and the Invisible* intended to elaborate such an idea of philosophy, Merleau-Ponty writes that the latter "shows by words. Like all literature."[47] Therefore, according to this idea, philosophy, just as contemporary literature, tends to tie a "new bond" with the visible, through which it would be able to *sichtbar machen*, that is, "make visible."

How, then, does Merleau-Ponty envision this "showing by words" that characterizes philosophy by highlighting its proximity to literature? In order to clarify what in *The Visible and the Invisible* he calls—with a term that is consciously inadequate—the "object" of philosophy, Merleau-Ponty explains that the "effective, present, ultimate and primary being, the thing itself, are in principle *apprehended in transparency* through their perspectives, offer themselves therefore only to someone who wishes not *to have them* but *to see them*, not to hold them as with forceps, or to immobilize them as under the objective of a microscope, but *to let them be* and to witness their continued being—to someone who therefore limits himself to giving them the hollow, the free space they ask for in return, the resonance they require."[48]

In this dense passage, the attitude of philosophy in relation to its "object" is discussed in terms of "seeing," which is understood in a way that is similar to the one I identified above as a *seconding from within*. In fact, such a way of seeing implies the renunciation of the claims to the *Begriff*'s intellectual possession[49]—that is, of the concept in its modern meaning—and is in fact one and the same with a "letting-be." Such an expression—which is not the only sign of an Heideggerian inspiration in this text—is repeated a few lines farther on, in order to designate perception itself, where the latter is significantly defined likewise as an "interrogative thought": "It is necessary to comprehend perception as this interrogative thought which lets the perceived world be rather than posits it, before which the things form and undo themselves in a sort of gliding, beneath the yes and the no."[50]

In this light, we can therefore assert that in the characterization of philosophy as a "showing by words," the seeing implied here has to be understood as an equivalent of "apprehending in transparency" the thinking of the sensible—or the *logos* of the aesthetic world—*letting it be* (the "listening eye" is precisely the eye letting be), and thus giving back to it—in a never achieved phenomenological reduction—precisely "the resonance it requires." As a "showing by words," language is indeed the resonance of the silence in which the sensible dwells, and on which language itself feeds. Thus, language cannot claim to observe from the outside, it cannot claim not to be implicated, because, according to Merleau-Ponty, not even philosophical language "reabsorbs its own contingency, and wastes away to make the things themselves appear."[51]

"Showing by words" is thus *seconding from within* the manifestation of the sensible logos[52] through the work of *creation* of the words themselves, manifesting, at the same time, the fact of *being part* of such a logos [*d'en être*].

In the course notes we have examined, Merleau-Ponty judges that art and literature—prior to and more effectively than philosophy—have succeeded in expressing the "mutation in the relationship between humanity and Being" that he finds at work in our epoch. This is because, in other words, modern art and literature, according to Merleau-Ponty, have been capable—prior to and more effectively than philosophy—to *second* the showing of the sensible *from within*, *letting be* its peculiar "logic of implication or promiscuity,"[53] in which "every relation with being is *simultaneously* a taking and a being taken."[54] In other words, modern art and literature succeeded in avoiding to superimpose to such a logic the antithetical logic of representation, which for the most part still remains dominant in philosophy. In fact, the classic logic of seeing understood as a representing by frontal positioning is precisely what still underlies the notion of concept according to which the subject *grasps* in thought the universal representation of the object positioned in front of it.

In the last page of "The Philosopher and His Shadow," Merleau-Ponty seems to provide the emblem of this logic of representation[55] in the (supposed) representative frontality of the Renaissance perspective. On the other hand, he assimilates the being of the sensible to a "Baroque world" (and here, following Deleuze, we could find once again Paul Klee).[56] In this world, in fact, Merleau-Ponty sees a "configurational meaning which is in no way indicated by its 'theoretical meaning'"[57] (which has to be understood as a *kosmotheoretical* meaning).

In the essay titled "Everywhere and Nowhere," also collected in *Signs*,[58] Merleau-Ponty goes so far as to state that the "philosophical problem" of our epoch is "to open the concept without destroying it,"[59] in order to conserve, as he suggests a little further on, its "rigor,"[60] while abandoning the pretension to the "intellectual possession of the world."[61] Maybe then this "opening" of the concept should be thought along the lines of the baroque configuration of the sensible, according to which every taking is simultaneously a being taken and feeling is in reality a letting-be. In this way, we would renounce the claims of the *Begriff* to take "intellectual possession of the world," and we would enable conceptuality to speak, at last, about "the passivity of our activity," of which, as it is highlighted in a working note of *The Visible and the Invisible*, "[p]hilosophy has never spoken."[62]

Thus, it is no accident that precisely in a discussion about a theorist of the Baroque we are reminded that the term *concept*, in its Latin etymology, had a certain semantic halo whose traces can be discerned in the direction of thinking that Merleau-Ponty seems to indicate. In fact, while in the German word *Begriff*, "the act of comprehension is etymologically bound to the *greifen*, i.e., to prehension meant as grasping, in the Latin word *conceptus*, on the contrary, the act of comprehension is etymologically derived from *cum-capio*, which means 'taking' in the sense of 'welcoming.'"[63] Such would be a *taking together*, a taking that is *simultaneously* a being taken. In this sense, to understand would not mean to take possession of something, but rather to "second" its manifestation from within. In the same direction, we could find this same alternative in the terms Jacques Taminiaux used to characterize the Kantian imagination as a creator of aesthetic ideas: "To create is not to act in the sense of subjecting. Rather, it is to consent," which etymologically means "to feel together."[64]

Chapter Four

The Philosopher and the Moviemaker

Merleau-Ponty and Cinematic Thinking

Making Seen Instead of Explaining: The Historical Convergence of Cinema and Philosophy

In 1948 Merleau-Ponty collects in the volume *Sense and Non-Sense*[1] his main articles written during the previous years, and divides them into three parts respectively titled *"Oeuvres"* (in English translated as "Arts"), "Ideas," and "Politics."

In the four texts composing the first section, which were previously published between 1945 and 1947, Merleau-Ponty highlights the deep convergence of certain artistic experiences and both the psychology he characterizes as "new"—which he tends to identify with the Gestalt Psychology—and contemporary philosophy. The artistic experiences Merleau-Ponty focuses on are painting in "Cézanne's Doubt"; cinema in "The Film and the New Psychology"; and literature, both in "Metaphysics and the Novel"—which comments on Simone de Beauvoir's *She Came to Stay*—and in "A Scandalous Author," written to defend Sartre.

Merleau-Ponty sees such convergence manifested in the themes concerning our relation to the world and our relation to the others. As for the first theme, Merleau-Ponty opens "The Film and the New Psychology"[2]— which is the text of the lecture given in 1945 at the Institut des Hautes Études Cinématographiques (IDHEC) of Paris—by pointing out that the psychology he characterizes as "classical" tends to attribute a primary role, in our sensible knowledge, to *sensations*, meant as the *punctual* effects of as many local excitements that intelligence and memory would *successively* have the task of composing in a unitary picture. Instead, as Merleau-Ponty highlights, the "new psychology" shows that what should be considered as *primary* is *perception*, understood as the sensible apprehension of a phenomenon as a whole: "analytical perception, through which we arrive at absolute value of the separate elements, is a belated and rare attitude—that of the scientist who observes or of the philosopher who reflects. The perception of forms, understood very broadly as structure, grouping, or configuration should be considered our spontaneous way of seeing."[3]

On this basis, the "new psychology" points out the synesthetic characteristic of perception, in virtue of which perception shall not be considered as "a sum of visual, tactile, and audible givens,"[4] for it "speaks to all my senses at once."[5] More generally, Merleau-Ponty judges that, "[b]y resolutely rejecting the notion of sensation," the theory of form (*Gestalttheorie*) "teaches us to stop distinguishing between signs and their significance, between what is sensed and what is judged."[6]

Also in the case of the theme concerning our relation to the others, Merleau-Ponty considers that the "new psychology" brings a "new concept" of their *perception*, on the basis of which one shall reject "the distinction between inner observation, or introspection, and outer observation."[7] Indeed, "we must reject that prejudice which makes 'inner realities' out of love, hate or anger, leaving them accessible to one single witness: the person who feels them."[8] In fact, according to Merleau-Ponty, the "new psychology" shows that "[a]nger, shame, hate, and love are not psychic facts hidden at the bottom of another's consciousness: they are types of behavior or styles of conduct which are visible from the outside."[9]

Merleau-Ponty claims that "the best observation of the aestheticians of the cinema"[10] converges with such novelties in psychology. He makes every effort to highlight them by considering "film as a perceptual object,"[11] that is, as explained by Enzo Paci in his "Introduction" to the Italian translation of *Sense and Non-Sense*, by considering "cinema [. . .] as a moving form (meant as *Gestalt*)."[12]

On this subject, Merleau-Ponty specifies that "a film is not a sum total of images, but a temporal *Gestalt*."[13] Within this temporal *Gestalt*, which is essentially characterized by its *rhythm*, "the meaning of a shot therefore depends on what precedes it in the movie, and this succession of scenes creates a new reality which is not merely the sum of its parts."[14]

On the basis of such a definition, Merleau-Ponty describes a famous, and yet lost, cinematic sequence that he attributed to Vsevolod Pudovkin, but which had actually been realized by his master Lev Kuleshov, namely the founder, with Dziga Vertov, of Soviet cinema. In this sequence, Kuleshov meant to account for the creative role of montage, which he considered to be cinema's main form of expression.

"One day Pudovkin took a close-up of Mosjoukin with a completely impassive expression and projected it after showing: first, a bowl of soup, then, a young woman lying dead in her coffin, and, last, a child playing with a teddy-bear. The first thing noticed was that Mosjoukin seemed to be looking at the bowl, the young woman, and the child, and the next one noted that he was looking pensively at the dish, that he wore an expression of sorrow when looking at the woman, and that he had a glowing smile for the child. The audience was amazed at his variety of expression although the same shot had actually been used all three times and was, if anything, remarkably inexpressive."[15]

In the fine essay in which he comments on Merleau-Ponty's text,[16] Pierre Rodrigo identifies the above quoted passage as "the heart of the lecture's reasoning,"[17] reporting that the reference to "this *specific* feature of cinematic art, i.e., montage,"[18] opens up within such reasoning "an evident lacuna: nothing is said about the significative power of image *as such*."[19] This is how, according to him, the Merleau-Pontian reasoning reveals image "as the *atom* of meaning with which montage has to be involved—just like the *word* is the atom of meaning in classical linguistics."[20] Because of this, Rodrigo stresses, by absolutizing the teaching of Soviet mute cinema, such reasoning focuses precisely on montage, that is to say on the meaning as it emerges *among* images, just like—within a sentence—it emerges *among* words. Instead, he claims that—when recognized in its expressive complexity, which will be enhanced by sound cinema—"a cinematic image is a sentence, not merely a word."[21]

Sure enough, Rodrigo's claim can be shared fully. However, the reasoning developed by Merleau-Ponty in the IDHEC lecture seems to be supported by many good arguments.

Let us leave aside the fact that the privilege accorded by Soviet mute cinema to montage is no more questionable than the obsession for long takes—recalled by Rodrigo[22]—which the founder of the *Cahiers du cinéma* and spiritual father of the *Nouevelle vague* André Bazin sets up against it. Still, it remains to be remarked, first of all, that such a privilege appears particularly useful for the goal declared in Merleau-Ponty's lecture, that is, to show that "we can apply what we have just said about perception in general to the perception of a film,"[23] a goal which the lecture itself clearly expresses in the beginning of its second half, shifting the reflection from "new psychology" to cinema. Indeed, it is true that this second half does not really limit itself to "applying to the film perception" the psychological principles explained in the first half, and it is true that, on the contrary, by confronting cinema, it "retrospectively transforms everything which could be said until then."[24] However, it is no less true that cinematic montage appears as a particularly effective example of that characteristic of novelty of *Gestaltpsychologie*, with which Merleau-Ponty began his discussion: "groups rather than juxtaposed elements are principal and primary in our perception."[25]

On the other hand, straight after having expressed such a characteristic, he provided not only visual but also auditory examples, focusing them on the gestaltist example of melody. And this is Bergsonian,[26] before even being Gestaltist. As Merleau-Ponty writes, "[t]he melody is not a sum of notes, since each note only counts by virtue of the function it serves in the whole [. . .]. Such a perception of the whole is more natural and more primary than the perception of isolated elements."[27]

And the example of melody is precisely the one Merleau-Ponty refers to when he comes to talk about the Kuleshov effect. He in fact introduces it by pointing out that it "clearly shows the *melodic* unity of films,"[28] for he is interested in highlighting that the film, just like a musical melody, is "a temporal *gestalt*."[29]

Therefore, differently from what Rodrigo's criticism suggests, it seems to me that, while commenting on the Kuleshov effect, Merleau-Ponty does not have in mind the assimilation of the single cinematic image to the verbal atom of a sentence, but rather *to an isolated musical note*. However, considering such a note in this way indeed appears abstract. On the other hand, even the main character of the first volume of Proust's *Recherche*, Swann, understood this issue in the pages Merleau-Ponty recalled in *Phenomenology of Perception*,[30] which was published in the same year in which the lecture at the IDHEC was given. In those pages Proust wrote: "[w]hen [. . .] he [i.e., Swann] had sought to disentangle from his confused impressions how it was that it [i.e., the little phrase] swept over and enveloped him, he had observed that it was to the closeness of the intervals between the five notes which composed it and to the constant repetition of two of them that was due that impression of a frigid and withdrawn sweetness; but in reality he knew that he was basing this conclusion not upon the phrase itself, but merely upon certain equivalents, substituted (for his mind's convenience) for the mysterious entity of which he had become aware [. . .] when for the first time he had heard the sonata played."[31]

Hence, not differently from Swann, Merleau-Ponty knows that he would never come across what really gives sense to the considered expressive unity—the little musical phrase in one case, the cinematic sequence in the other—if he disassembled its "form" (i.e., *Gestalt*) in order to analyze its single components. In fact, as we have already heard him explain, "analytical perception, through which we arrive at absolute value of the separate elements, is a belated and rare attitude—that of the scientist who observes or of the philosopher who reflects,"[32] as well as, we might add, that of the specialist in aesthetics or cinema. Precisely for this reason, by considering the Kuleshov effect, Merleau-Ponty means to focus on "the perception of forms, understood very broadly as structure, grouping, or configuration [which] should be considered our spontaneous way of perceiving."[33]

Implicitly, Merleau-Ponty then contributes to freeing cinema from the heavy claim staked by Henri Bergson when the "seventh art" was but ten years old, with the famous judgment he expressed in the fourth chapter of *Creative Evolution*. Here Bergson had in turn drawn a parallel between our perception and the working of cinema, but in such a way as to disavow the knowledge of becoming that both our perception and the working of cinema claimed to offer us: "Such is the contrivance of the cinematograph. And such is also that of our knowledge. Instead of attaching ourselves to the inner becoming of things, we place ourselves outside them in order to recompose their becoming artificially. We take snapshots, as it were, of the passing reality, and, as these are characteristic of the reality, we have only to string them on a becoming, abstract, uniform and invisible, situated at the back of the apparatus of knowledge, in order to imitate what there is that is characteristic in this becoming itself. Perception, intellection, language, so proceed in general. Whether we would think becoming, or express it, or even perceive it, we hardly do anything else than set going a kind of cinematograph inside us. We may therefore sum up what we have been saying in the conclusion that the *mechanism of our ordinary knowledge is of a cinematographical kind*."[34]

If understood literally, this claim could also summarize the meaning of Merleau-Ponty's lecture, in which he indeed affirms that "we can apply what we have just said about perception in general to the perception of a film." But it is evident that Merleau-Ponty can come to a conclusion so similar to that of Bergson only *by reversing* its premises: our spontaneous perception is not analytic, but synthetic, and *precisely for this reason* it can be considered "cinematographical" by nature. In fact, within its synthetic character we find at work dynamics which are essential for providing us with the *unity* of a perceived form as well as that of a cinematic sequence: far from being "artificial," as Bergson tends to define them, they contribute instead to the *truth* of our perceptions.

In the light of this, the reason why Merleau-Ponty's lecture does not focus on "the significative power of image *as such*," to recall the terms of Rodrigo's criticism, may be better understood. Indeed, to focus on such power would be to miss that *specificity* of the cinematic expression which does not consist so much in montage—which, instead, is a consequence of this specificity—but rather in its characteristic of "temporal *Gestalt*." Also by means of his remark on the Kuleshov effect, Merleau-Ponty's aim is such specificity: this is why he avoids focusing on "image as such," for precisely focusing on it would make it become that "atomic" element Rodrigo blames him for reducing image to.

Instead, the characterization of film assumed by Merleau-Ponty, far from making him lose his attention to images, leads him to highlight how much "the time-factor for each shot"[35] means to the film itself, to remind us that "the alternation of words and silence is manipulated to create the most effective image,"[36] to focus, in a word, on the "internal rhythm of the scene," as we may say recalling the phrase used by Maurice Jaubert.[37]

Indeed, according to such a characterization of film, as Jean-Pierre Charcosset explains, "the perception of an image [. . .] itself depends upon the perception of the sequence in which it is integrated. So far that the same shot is perceived in a different way depending on the shots that precede it and on those that follow it. But such a *Gestalt* is temporal not only insofar as its projection 'requires time,' but most of all insofar as the sense of a shot varies depending on its duration. From which, a first consequence: the sense of a film depends less on the images of which it is composed than on the *rhythm* of its images."[38]

Such a consequence implicates another, which consists in revealing the fictional characteristic underlying the film's apparent realism. "[W]hat supports this ambiguity is the fact that movies do have a basic realism," Merleau-Ponty remarks. "That does not mean, however, that the movies are fated to let us see and hear what we would see and hear if we were present at the events being related."[39] Both the fictional characteristic and the apparent realism of the film are read according to a perspective explicitly referring to Kant's aesthetics. In particular, the reference concerns the definition of "aesthetic ideas" formulated in § 49 of the *Critique of the Power of Judgment*. Elaborated by the artist's imagination and embodied in the beauty of the artwork he created, aesthetic ideas occasion "much thinking,"[40] without being completely conceptualizable and conceptually expressible. In the case of cinema, according to Merleau-Ponty's interpretation, this means that the sense "of a film is incorporated to its rhythm just as the meaning of a gesture may immediately be read in that gesture: the film doesn't mean anything but itself. The idea is presented in a nascent state,"[41] that is to say, in its unconceptualized form. As a consequence, the idea turns out being indiscernible from its sensible manifestation: "[it] emerges from the temporal structure of the film as it does from the coexistence of the parts of a painting. [. . .] [A] movie has meaning in the same way that a thing does: neither of them speaks to an isolated understanding; rather, both appeal to our power tacitly to decipher the world or men and to coexist with them."[42]

Here reemerges Merleau-Ponty's conviction concerning the intimate convergence between the "new psychology" and certain artistic and philosophical tendencies of the same epoch. Their mutual intention seems to be that of *teaching us anew how to see the world*, as we may say following the famous statement by which Husserl defined the fundamental phenomenological task, and which Merleau-Ponty echoed precisely to describe the aim of the "new psychology": "it re-educates us in how to see the world which we touch at every point of our being."[43] Further on, the echo of the Husserlian statement returns in terms that can significantly be referred to Proust's literary experience or to Paul Klee's pictorial experience. In fact, in the first volume of the *Recherche*, Proust wrote apropos of the "little phrase" of Vinteuil's sonata: "Those graces of an intimate sorrow, 'twas them that the phrase endeavoured to imitate, to create anew; and even their essence, for all that it consists in being incommunicable and in appearing trivial to everyone save him who has experience of them, the little phrase had captured, had *rendered visible*."[44] As we know, it is by this very expression that Klee opened his *Creative Credo*: "Art does not reproduce the visible; rather, it makes visible." For his part, Merleau-Ponty moves toward the conclusion of his lecture on "The Film and the New Psychology" by suggesting an idea of philosophy that anticipates the one we came across in the previous chapter when quoting a working note of *The Visible and the Invisible*: "Phenomenological or existential philosophy is largely an expression of surprise at this inherence of the self in the world and in others, a description of this paradox and permeation, and an attempt to make us *see* the bond between subject and world, between subject and others, rather than to *explain* it as the classical philosophies did by resorting to absolute spirit."[45]

We have already mentioned the fact that Merleau-Ponty's lecture is divided into two parts: one is devoted to the new psychology, the other to cinema, and each is typographically distinguished. A similar typographical separation signals the end of the second half and heralds its conclusions. It is precisely in the conclusions that the above quoted sentence appears.

Here, the two conceptual characters that had until then shared the scene, are joined by a third character, which had previously kept a spectator's position: such a character is indeed philosophy. Or, more precisely, the "contemporary philosophies,"[46] whose inspiration is there described as in spontaneous and yet specific syntony with those of the "new psychology" and cinema. Therefore, by contrast, Bergson's philosophy is evoked. In fact, even if it is never mentioned during the lecture, it is precisely such philosophy which seems to have suggested to Merleau-Ponty the very choice, at first peculiar, of presenting the acquisitions of "modern psychology"[47] to an audience of moviemakers to come, so as to get to confute in front of them the dismissive Bergsonian judgment on cinema.

Instead, here is "contemporary philosophy"—Merleau-Ponty now declines this in the singular—recognizing itself in motivations, interests and styles of research that are in agreement with those of the "new psychology" and cinema: particularly with those of cinema for—as he explains—contemporary philosophy "consists not in stringing concepts together but in describing the mingling of consciousness with the world, its involvement in a body, and its coexistence with others; and [. . .] this is movie material *par excellence.*"[48]

Retrospectively reasoning, in 1968 the French semiologist and historian of cinema Christian Metz will remark: "Following Merleau-Ponty's lecture on 'Le Cinéma et la nouvelle psychologie,' film began to be defined here and there, or at least approached, from what one called the 'phenomenological' angle: a sequence of film, like a spectacle from life, carries its meaning within itself. The signifier is not easily distinguished from the significate. This is an entirely new concept of ordering. The cinema is the 'phenomenological' art *par excellence*, the signifier is coextensive with the whole of the significate, the spectacle its own signification, thus short-circuiting the sign itself."[49]

Metz then composes a long list of those who were influenced by such a conception: "This is what was said, in substance, by Souriau, Soriano, Blanchard, Marcel, Cohen-Séat, Bazin, Martin, Ayfre, Astre, Cauliez, Dort, Vailland, Marion, Robbe-Grillet, B. and R. Zazzo and many others [. . .] It is possible, even probable, that they went too far in this direction: for the cinema is after all not life; it is a created spectacle. But let us put these reservations aside for the moment, and simply record what was in fact a convergence in the historical evolution of ideas about film."[50]

It is not difficult to recognize in the perspective that Metz finds drawn by Merleau-Ponty's lecture some of the features that, with greater evidence, have meanwhile come to typify the *Nouvelle Vague* cinema. Therefore, it is not surprising to find in a film by its most emblematic *auteur* a quotation of the sentence by which Merleau-Ponty, coming to the conclusion of his lecture, already identified that "convergence" we heard Metz echo almost twenty years later: "The philosopher and the moviemaker share a certain way of being, a certain view of the world which belongs to a generation."[51]

The film in which this sentence appears is *Masculin Féminin*;[52] its author, as everybody knows, is Jean-Luc Godard, and it was distributed in 1966. In that same year Robert Bresson's *Au Hasard, Balthazar* was also released in France and, in issue 177 of the *Cahiers du cinéma*, a text titled "Le testament de Balthazar" was published. It appeared to be composed of "collected statements" ["*propos recueillis*"] written by Godard himself together with Merleau-Ponty:[53] to the innocent donkey, protagonist of Bresson's film, are attributed reflections on time, otherness, death, cogito, and freedom. In some of them it is easy to recognize passages taken from the *Phenomenology of Perception*, which, as we know, is coeval with the IDHEC lecture. When he appears as signee of "Le testament de Balthazar," Merleau-Ponty had been dead for five years.

The Question of Motion in Cinema

But let us go back to Merleau-Ponty's sentence concerning the generational convergence of the philosopher and the moviemaker that will excite Godard's enthusiasm, and let us try to trace its developments within the ulterior Merleau-Pontian reflection.

Only fifteen years after Merleau-Ponty had written this sentence, such a prudent and, to be frank, narrow generational hypothesis will end up being modified in an ontological sense. We see Merleau-Ponty going in such a direction in the preparatory notes for the unfinished course titled "Cartesian Ontology and the Ontology of Today." These notes present the course, highlighting that the subject after which it is titled "[i]s not the history of philosophy in the current sense: what has been thought, it is: what has been thought in the context and the horizon of what one thinks—Evoked in order to understand what one thinks. Rather: Contemporary ontology—Starting from this, then towards Descartes and Cartesians, and back to what philosophy can be today."[54]

Actually, this course aims at helping to provide contemporary ontology with a philosophical formulation. Apropos of contemporary ontology—that "spontaneous philosophy, fundamental thinking" which, as we already read, has so far been expressed "especially in literature,"[55] but also in the arts—Merleau-Ponty specifies in parentheses "(painting-cinema)."[56] A couple of lines farther he adds: "André Bazin ontology of cinema [*André Bazin ontologie du cinéma*]"[57]; and once more, a little farther on: "In the arts / Cinema ontology of cinema—example the question of movement in cinema [*Dans les arts / Cinéma ontologie du cinéma—Ex. la question du mouvement au cinéma*]."[58]

The notes of this course, hence, promised to pick out, in the experiences and the reflections developed by cinema, some tendency lines converging with those sketched by coeval painting and literature in tracing the outline of the "new ontology," which Merleau-Ponty planned "to try to formulate philosophically"[59] precisely with this course. As we read, it was his particular intention to point out such tendency lines by way of assuming as *exemplum*, "the question of movement in cinema." It is no surprise then—but appears all the more interesting—that the only two further traces of the later Merleau-Ponty's reflections on cinema concern precisely such a question.

One of these traces can be found in a chapter of *The Visible and the Invisible*, which Merleau-Ponty himself will replace with another version, and which thus appears as an "appendix" in the posthumous volume edited by Claude Lefort. The trace I am alluding to is composed by a few intricate lines, in the first part of which the reasons for the Bergsonian condemnation of cinema seem to be echoed critically: "The discontinuous images of the cinema prove nothing with regard to the phenomenal truth of the movement that connects them before the eyes of the spectator—moreover, they do not even prove that the life world involves movements without a mobile: the mobile could well be projected by him who perceives."[60]

The other trace of the later Merleau-Ponty's reflections on cinema lies within the comparison between the various artistic expressions of movement he develops in *Eye and Mind*. Here he writes that "Marey's photographs, the cubists' analyses, Duchamp's *La Mariée* do not move; they give a Zenonian reverie on movement. We see a rigid body as if it were a piece of armor going through its motions; it is here and it is there, magically, but it does not *go* from here to there. Cinema portrays movement, but *how*? It is, as we are inclined to believe, by copying more closely the changes of place? We may presume not, since slow motion shows a body being carried along, floating among objects like seaweed, but not *moving itself*."[61] Merleau-Ponty thus emphasizes the *nonmimetic* feature of film realism—the ontological significance of such a remark is evident here—even without developing further his references to cinema.

However, Merleau-Ponty had lingered a bit longer on "the use of movement in painting and cinematic art"[62] in the summary of the first course he gave at the Collège de France, once again taking interest in their confluent features. It is the 1952–53 course devoted to "The Sensible World and the World of Expression," the preparatory notes for which have been transcribed and edited by Emmanuel de Saint Aubert[63] and by Stefan Kristensen.[64]

The reflections Merleau-Ponty provides in this course allow us to realize—or at least indicate more precisely—the directions in which the later phase of his thought could have developed an ontological conception of cinema. Moreover, the notes prepared for the course "The Sensible World and the World of Expression" seem to support retrospectively the interpretation of the lecture Merleau-Ponty gave at the IDHEC as a silently polemic response to the Bergsonian judgment on cinema. In fact, just as in "The Cinema and the New Psychology," in these notes Merleau-Ponty discusses perception on the basis of the *Gestalttheorie*, and such a basis is used, this time explicitly, in order to reject Bergson's positions on cinema.

On the other hand, the summary of this same course already showed that Merleau-Ponty resorted to the *Gestalt* research in order to feed his opposition toward the Bergsonian thesis on movement, an opposition that seems to account for some of the allusions we found in the rewritten chapter of *The Visible and the Invisible*. Indeed, in this summary, he explained as follows: "motion as a change in location or variation in the relations between a 'mobile' and its coordinates is a retrospective schema, an ulterior formulation of our carnal experience of movement. Once motion is cut off from its perceptual origins, it defies representation and is self-destructive, as has often been shown since Zeno. But to give an intelligible account of motion it is not enough to go back, as suggested by Bergson, to the internal experience of motion, in other words, to our *own* movement. We have to understand how the immediate unity of our gesture is able to spread itself over external experiences and introduce into them the possibility of transition which from the standpoint of objective thought is unreal."[65]

It is precisely when facing this question that Merleau-Ponty resorts to "the research in Gestalt theory."[66] And it is precisely when facing this question that, as I mentioned before, in the notes to the same course he critically echoes Bergson's positions on cinema in the light of Max Wertheimer's descriptions concerning stroboscopic movement. Wertheimer was the main Gestaltist theorist, and the stroboscopic movement he discussed is the apparent movement that is produced by the rapid succession of images on a background, which allows the viewer to perceive in a unitary way a cinematic sequence. But beware: according to Merleau-Ponty, such an experience cannot lead us to suppose any "movement without a mobile." This latter formulation, which is dismissed in the second part of the short reference to cinema featured in the "appendix" of *The Visible and the Invisible*, is echoed several times in these 1952–53 course notes,[67] where it is indeed attributed to Wertheimer. In recalling the remarks already developed in *Phenomenology of Perception*, Merleau-Ponty considers such a formulation to be indefensible, risking to make movement once more inconceivable, for in any case "he must be referring to an identical something that moves."[68] Therefore, these notes object to Wertheimer no less than to Bergson the exigency of a "theory of the perceiving body."[69] Indeed, only such a theory could attest to the "phenomenal truth of the movement" produced by "the discontinuous images of the cinema," hence showing us—this is the sense of the words we encountered in the short passage of the "appendix" to *The Visible and the Invisible*—that "the mobile could well be projected by him who perceives." Besides, this latter formulation, written in a subjectivist language, would be sufficient to explain Merleau-Ponty's decision not to publish this chapter. However, what is most important is to retain the Merleau-Pontian exigency of affirming, by the reference to corporeity, the immediate inscription of movement *both on the exterior and on the interior side of our experience.* For the same purpose, in the 1952–1953 course notes, Merleau-Ponty uses the notion of "figural" in order to designate certain indecomposable features proper to *our perception* of a figure on a ground, and *not to the figure on the ground as such*, as the *Gestaltpsychologie* claimed. In short, he used this term so as to account for the essentially unitary characteristic of our experience of movement, while in his opinion "[t]he *Gestalt* turns figural moments into objective conditions, which determine a process of organization in the third person according to causality laws."[70]

Let us then quote Kristensen, who refers to the notes he transcribed in order to explain that, according to Merleau-Ponty, "[t]he structure of the stroboscopic movement coincides with that of our 'natural perception.' [. . .] There is an essential affinity between the functioning of our visual perception and the production of movement by cinematic technique. To support this idea, he indeed evokes cinema. The cinematic device is 'in no way illusion,' he writes with reference to the well-known Bergsonian thesis of the *Creative Evolution* in the beginning of the fourth chapter. It must be admitted that [. . .] our body [. . .] shapes the perceived according to a structure that is its own."[71]

In order to support his thesis, Merleau-Ponty makes some direct references to one of the very rare movies he mentions in these course notes. More precisely, he refers to a specific sequence of *Zéro de conduite* (in English: *Zero for Conduct*), a masterpiece by the French film director Jean Vigo that was first issued on April 7, 1933, and was subsequently banned in France until 1945. The film is now considered a classic, and was particularly admired by the exponents of the *Nouvelle Vague*. Merleau-Ponty focuses on the famous sequence of the boys' nighttime rebellion in the dormitory of their boarding school. In the first part of this sequence, all the objects in the dormitory are thrown around as the children express their disdain for authority. Partway through the sequence, there is a shift to slow motion as pillows and feathers fly, and the children parade through the room. As Georges Sadoul observed, this sequence is remarkable "not only for its music, but also for the symphony in white major of its images."[72] All of Merleau-Ponty's allusions to the sequence in his working notes are accompanied by the reference to a name in parenthesis: that of Maurice Jaubert. Before the Second World War, Jaubert was the most important French composer of film music. His reflections on "the role of music" in a movie was quoted by Merleau-Ponty in *The Film and the New Psychology*.[73] Jaubert also composed the music for *Zéro de conduite*. About the sequence quoted by Merleau-Ponty, Jaubert himself had explained as follows: "The composer had to accompany a procession of rebellious children (quite ghostly in fact and shot in slow motion). Once the necessary music was obtained and wanting to use an unreal sonorousness, he transcribed it backwards, the last bar before the first and within each bar, the last note before the first. The bit of music in this form was then recorded and recalled little of the original music. The music thus obtained was then used with the film and one found again the shape of the basic melody but the 'trasmission' was entirely reversed and derived all its mystery from this simple mechanical operation."[74]

Merleau-Ponty's notes refer precisely to the effect produced at once by the reversal of the original music and the use of slow motion. Besides, his notes seem to echo Jaubert's explication itself, for they highlight in turn the "impression of irreality,"[75] of "strangeness [?]"[76] that the sequence causes in the spectator. We can hence understand Merleau-Ponty's interest in this sequence. In it, he sees a sort of negative proof, a sort of evidence to the contrary, showing the existence of a *logic shared* by our average perception and by the cinematic perception, despite Bergson's opinion according to which the latter was just an illusory reproduction of the former. By reversing the sounds and making the motion slow, this sequence from *Zéro de conduite tries to elude* precisely that *perceptive logic*,[77] thus producing an effect of derealization. This is why, in the summary of Merleau-Ponty's course, we can read the following passage: "The quality of the sound from a wind instrument bears the mark and the organic rhythm of the breath from which it came, as can be shown by the strange impression received by reversing the normal register of the sounds. Far from being a simple 'displacement,' movement is inscribed in the texture of the shapes or qualities and is, so to speak, the revelation of their being."[78]

There is more. When observing this sequence, it becomes evident that it is precisely to it that Merleau-Ponty will make reference, more or less eight years later, in the already mentioned passage from *Eye and Mind*, in which, talking about the cinematic expression of movement, he will claim—actually a bit mysteriously—that "slow motion shows a body being carried along, floating among objects like seaweed, but not *moving itself*."[79] In the sequence in question, that body floating as seaweed appears, while its somersault slowly soars in the air as if that body itself was a feather. Or as if one of Bill Viola's angels.[80]

Reread within the context of images and reflections that I just tried to recall, that sentence from *Eye and Mind* is then confirmed once and for all as a claim which, far from meaning to disavow the perception of movement offered by cinema, rather criticizes the idea that the more such a perception is left to a close reproduction of movement itself, the more it is realistic. On the contrary, a close reproduction of movement cannot but distort the perceptive logic that immediately joins our body to the world. Therefore, our body will not recognize, in the slow motion projected movements of a similar body, the acting of its double. Rather, it will believe it is observing a way of dwelling in the world that is completely different from its own, as that of seaweed can be. It is thus precisely because this perceptive logic shows that we are joined to the world in an immediate and essential way, that it prevents us from separating the consideration of movement as we experience it and as it takes place in the world. Such a logic should even prevent us from describing it as a movement that is *within Being*, if by this expression we keep meaning that Being remains motionless. Indeed, as the Gestaltist experiments show and as the experiences of cinema confirm, *the background essentially participates in the perception of movement*, imposing us to characterize such a movement not as movement *in* Being, but rather as movement *of* Being itself, which in its turn is revealed as *being movement*. This is precisely what the course notes in question end up pointing out: "Therefore here movement = revelation of Being, outcome of its internal configuration and clearly different from change of place."[81]

Hence, according to Merleau-Ponty, cinema helps to indicate the direction to be followed in order to avoid the fundamental dualisms of the Western tradition. In this sense, the summary of the course, "The Sensibile World and the World of Expression," proposes some reflections making the "use of movement" issue coincide not merely with a particular question, but with the very identity of what we heard Merleau-Ponty call, with a remarkable expression, "cinematic art."

Merleau-Ponty had already referred to the question of cinema as art in his 1948 "Causeries" through the French radio: "Although cinema has not yet produced many works that are artworks through and through, although the infatuation with the movie stars, the sensational of the shot or of the vicissitudes changes, the interventions of beautiful photographs or of a spiritual dialogue are for the film just as many temptations in which it risks to embroil, finding success by omitting the ways of expression that are more proper to cinema—in spite of all these circumstances implying that so far we have not seen a film that is entirely a film, we still can glimpse what such a work would be, and we shall see that, as all works of art, it would be once more something we perceive."[82]

Merleau-Ponty thus suggests judging films as "artworks through and through," provided that they are "entirely films," namely, that they avoid the flatteries of commercial success just as much as those of other forms of expression, such as photography and literature, at the cost of its proper forms. In short, Merleau-Ponty suggests considering as "cinematic art" the cinema capable of being autonomous. In fact, the just quoted passage continues as follows: "what can constitute the cinematic beauty is not the story itself, which could be told well enough in prose, nor, and even more so, the ideas it may suggest, nor, finally, its tics, its manias—namely, those processes by which a director makes himself recognized and which have no more decisive importance than a writer's favorite words. What matters is the choice of the represented episodes, and, in each one of them, the choice of the images that will appear in the film, the length respectively attributed to each of these elements, the order in which one choses to present them, the sound or the words with which one means or not to accompany them, all of this would constitute a global cinematic rhythm."[83]

This "global cinematic rhythm" embodies precisely the "use of movement" that is proper to what Merleau-Ponty, in the course theme of "The Sensible World and the World of Expression," calls "cinematic art."[84]

In this course theme, he indeed writes that "[t]he cinema, invented as a means of photographing objects in movement or as a *representation of movement*, has discovered in the process much more than change in location, namely a new way of symbolizing thoughts, a *movement of representation*."[85]

In this very "discovery" seems to reside cinema's feature of "art," on the one hand—that is, the very nonmimetic feature Klee claimed for all art—and its ontological novelty, on the other hand. Both these features are more explicitly justified a little further, where Merleau-Ponty writes that "the film no longer plays with objective movements, as it did at first, but with *changes of perspective which define the shift from one person to another or his merging with the action*."[86]

It is also important to remark that, in the above-quoted sentence, Merleau-Ponty still uses the notion of "representation." However, it seems possible to affirm that the "discovery" defined in this sentence by the expression "movement of representation" is precisely what will lead him to abandon this notion so as to explore, in all of its implications, that of "vision," by resolutely refusing to reduce it, as we have already seen, to an "operation of thought that would set up before the mind a picture or a *representation* of the world."[87]

Furthermore, it seems that the reflections of Merleau-Ponty's interest toward André Bazin's observations—which were only mentioned in the 1960–61 course notes—can hence be better understood. In fact, the theoretical convergence between the later Merleau-Ponty and Bazin seem to develop a new ontological consideration of vision and thus of the image.

Ontology of the Image as Figure of Mutual Precession

On this issue, in his 1945 article on "The Ontology of the Photographic Image," which is considered to be fundamental for the renewal of the cinematic theories after World War II, by referring to the surrealist use of photography, Bazin wrote that "the logical distinction between what is imaginary and what is real tends to disappear. Every image is to be seen as an object and every object as an image."[88]

In *Eye and Mind*, when reflecting on the novelties of modern painting, Merleau-Ponty claims in his turn that the image shall no longer be considered as "a tracing [*décalque*], a copy, a second thing,"[89] more or less faithful to its model, and anyway produced by a vision independent from our sensible relation to the world.

Just like in the coeval pages of the unfinished *The Visibile and the Invisible*, here Merleau-Ponty thinks of the bodily experience as being constituted by the relational horizon cf the flesh.[90] He thus means to affirm the *rising* of vision from the very "core" of such a horizon, rather than describing it as *sticking out* from inside the body: "The visible about us seems to rest in itself. It is as though our vision were formed in the heart of the visible."[91]

Merleau-Ponty adds that what makes my vision rise at the core of the visible is the folding of the visible itself into a viewer. Indeed, in the same writing, Merleau-Ponty talks about "this *fold*, this central cavity of the visible which is my vision."[92] My experience of the body consists precisely in this "sort of folding back, invagination,"[93] a body experienced as a visible which is, at the same time, a viewer, as a sensible which is, at the same time, sentient. Such a condition is what makes me bear a relationship with the world that could be described as being like a kind of Möbius strip,[94] in virtue of which the sides traditionally defined as "inside" and "outside" trace the obverse and the reverse of the unique circle of vision.

Hence, in virtue of this circle, as Merleau-Ponty remarks in *Eye and Mind*, "we touch the sun and the stars, [. . .] we are everywhere at once, and [. . .] even our power to imagine ourselves elsewhere [. . .] or freely to envision real beings, wherever they are, borrows from vision and employs means we owe to it."[95]

In relation to that characterization of vision, in fact, the imaginary can neither be conceived of as a substituting faculty, nor a surrogate for reality; it does not express mere absence or total otherness with respect to the real. Rather, it turns out to germinate—precisely together with vision itself—from that *sensible kinship* between the world and us which, as we know, Merleau-Ponty calls "flesh." From this perspective, he infers that the imaginary is much closer to the "actual [*actuel*]"[96] than a *copy* of the actual itself would be, because in the imaginary the resonance that the actual elicits in the flesh of our sensible, affective, and symbolic relationship with the world finds itself expressed.

Hence, Merleau-Ponty writes, once again in *Eye and Mind*, that the pictorial image should be regarded, in its relation to the field of the actual, as its "pulp and carnal obverse exposed to view for the first time."[97] Still, can we avoid referring such a definition to the filmic experience itself?

At least, it is certain that Jean-Luc Godard cannot. In fact, in his film *JLG/JLG: Self-Portrait in December*, released in early 1995, he resorts to a few passages from a famous page of *The Visible and The Invisible*,[98] and assembles them in a *montage* resulting in a series of "phrases"—this is how the subtitle of the book released after the movie defines them—which

I can only partially quote: "if my left hand / can touch my right hand / while it palpates / the tangibles, / can touch it touching, / can turn its palpation back upon it . . ."[99]

Indeed, as Francesco Casetti points out in his book, significantly titled *Eye of the Century*,[100] cinema appears as the mode of expression that, being born in the same years as modern painting, has once and for all highlighted and made popular certain aspects of the "mutation within the relations of man and Being" that, in *Eye and Mind*, Merleau-Ponty spots precisely in modern painting. If, on the one hand, such relations can be negatively recognized in the refusal of the mimetic relation with the real, on the other hand, they seem to find a positive formulation in the definition of vision Merleau-Ponty provides in *Eye and Mind*, when he describes it as a "precession of what is upon what one sees and makes seen, of what one sees and makes seen upon what is."[101]

I am, hence, going to focus on this strange and complex formulation, as I feel it is quite rich in important implications. The word *precession*—which will become more current in the language of the French poststructuralist generation[102]—is only used on this single occasion in Merleau-Ponty's published texts, but I shall warmly thank Emmanuel de Saint Aubert for providing me with the list of all the passages in which the word appears in Merleau-Ponty's still unpublished manuscripts.[103]

Indeed, it appears for the first time in his reading notes, which were probably taken in 1957, on Rudolf Arnheim's *Art and Visual Perception: A Psychology of the Creative Eye*, namely, a book originally published in 1954,[104] where the word *precession*, however, was not mentioned. Later, it occurs several times in Merleau-Ponty's writings since 1960, starting with some drafts concerning the definition of vision from *Eye and Mind* I quoted above. On this basis, we can state that Merleau-Ponty seems to be interested in the word *precession* because it describes a *temporal* relation between the connected terms, rather than the *spatial* one suggested by the words *enjambement* and *empiétement*,[105] which, in those drafts, we find first put next to *precession* and then replaced with it.[106]

But the matter is not just Merleau-Ponty's preference for a temporal rather than a spatial relation. Indeed, the word *precession* describes a most peculiar temporality, which is characterized by a *movement of antecedence* of the concerned terms. This is the case with the precession of equinoxes, each of which happens about twenty minutes earlier each year.

Merleau-Ponty's preference for such a peculiar temporal relation becomes even more explicit in the unpublished "Large Summary" ["*Grand Résumé*" of *The Visible and the Invisible* prepared between November 1960 and May 1961. In particular, here we find the word *precession* in the following note written in the Fall of 1960: "Circularity, and *precession* visible-seer, silence-speech, I-Other [*moi-autrui*]."[107]

However, this formulation is significantly corrected in the following note from the same manuscript:

Circularity, but rather *precession*   visible-seer
                                           silence-speech
                                         I-Other [*moi-autrui*].[108]

In this same page of the "Large Summary," Merleau-Ponty tries to explain the meaning of the word precession by another astronomical expression: "gravitation of one around the other."[109] Such an expression indeed suggests a mutual—even if spatial—relation between the connected terms.

As for the formulation of *Eye and Mind*, it makes explicit this aspect of *mutuality* in a *temporal* way, since *precession* is characterized here precisely by a *movement of mutual anticipation* of the terms implied in this relation. In fact, Merleau-Ponty specifies: "This precession of what is upon what one sees and makes seen, of what one sees and makes seen upon what is—this is vision itself." It is precisely due to this *mutuality of anticipation* that Merleau-Ponty uses the word *precession* to describe the interrelations between "what is" and "what one sees and makes seen," which, in his opinion, define vision. In short, Merleau-Ponty's definition concerns a kind of precession that cannot be but *mutual*: that is, the precession of the gaze with regard to the things and of the things with regard to the gaze; the precession of the imaginary with regard to the "actual"—since the imaginary deems our gaze *making us see* the actual—and the precession of the "actual" with regard to the imaginary. This is how the primacy of a term rather than the other—the things or the gaze, the imaginary or the actual—becomes undecidable. In other words, we end up discarding the possibility of recognizing, once and for all, which term *comes first* and which one has to be considered, to recall Merleau-Ponty's expression, a "second thing." Besides, this should allow us to avoid keeping a "logical distinction"—this time the expression is Bazin's—between the movement and the mobile.[110]

In fact, the idea of mutual precession allows us to do without the notion of an absolute *before* in space and in time (or even of a "before" *of* space and *of* time). Therefore, it reveals how much our way of *thinking* about reality as *absolutely prior* is still metaphysical, and invites us to consider it differently.

Let us try to accept this invitation. Evidently, this mutual precession is a retrograde movement digging a peculiar kind of depth in time. On the same issue, in *Eye and Mind*, Merleau-Ponty evokes the "immemorial depth [*fond*] of the visible."[111] I believe it is precisely in this sense that such a temporal depth is to be thought. On this subject, once again referring to the Proustian *Recherche*, in a working note of *The Visible and the Invisible* dated April 1960, Merleau-Ponty wrote: "The Freudian idea of the unconscious and the past as 'indestructible,' as 'intemporal' = elimination of the common idea of time as a 'series of *Erlebnisse*'—There is an architectonic past. cf. Proust: the *true* hawthorns are the hawthorns of the past [. . .]. This 'past' belongs to a mythical time, to the time before time, to the prior life, 'farther than India and China.'"[112]

Moreover, in the manuscript of the same work he had already specified that this "mythical time" is the one "where certain events 'in the beginning' maintain a continued efficacy."[113] In my opinion, it is precisely the depth of this kind of time that is dug and instituted by the "precession of what is upon what one sees and makes seen, of what one sees and makes seen upon what is." Indeed, since this precession is infinitely mutual, it cannot bring us back to a chronological past. Rather, it can only bring us back to *a past that has never been present*, that is to say, a past which "belongs to a mythical time." This is the peculiar time at work in our unconscious, a time about whose indestructibility we read in the passage above. Similarly, "the indestructibility, [. . .] the transformability, and the anachronism of the *events* of memory" characterize, according to Didi-Huberman, this temporality,[114] which will be therefore related to an involuntary memory as that evoked precisely by Proust. In other words, in this peculiar temporality the experiences of our life are involuntarily elaborated, by a sort of "active oblivion,"[115] as "carnal essences,"[116] as "sensible ideas."[117] Such ideas are mythically retrojected and sedimented as such through what Bergson called "the retrograde movement of the true," thus always remaining at work in that "architectonic past." As I tried to show elsewhere,[118] the mythical time is hence the peculiar time in which live what Merleau-Ponty calls the "sensible ideas," suggesting by such a name not only that these ideas are inseparable from their sensible presentation (that is, from their visual, linguistic, or musical images, for instance),[119] but even that they are *instituted* by these very images as their own depth. Therefore, these images share that mythical temporality in which such ideas live. Concerning this subject, let us read the following passage from *Eye and Mind*: "Consider, as Sartre did in *Nausea*, the smile of a long-dead monarch which keeps producing and reproducing itself on

the surface of a canvas. It is too little to say that it is there as an image
or essence; it is there as itself, as that which was always most alive about
it, the moment I look at the painting.[120] The 'world's instant' that Cézanne
wanted to paint, an instant long since passed away, is still hurled toward
us by his paintings. His *Mont Sainte-Victoire* is made and remade from one
end of the world to the other in a way different from but no less energetic
than in the hard rock above Aix."[121]

Even though we saw that the later Merleau-Ponty's attention to cinema is explicitly focused on "the question of movement," I think that
the mythical time, on which he reflects mainly apropos of the Proustian
Recherche, is precisely *the time at work in the cinematic images*.[122] Without
such time, cinema would have not provided the twentieth century with
one of its most powerful myth systems and with its most popular place
for psychoanalytic elaboration. More generally, it seems to me that the
definition of vision elaborated by Merleau-Ponty in *Eye and Mind* ends up
characterizing the status the artistic experiences of the twentieth century
gradually accorded to images,[123] that is to say, the status of *mutual precession figures* rather than merely *figures referring to something else*. Cinema,
more than any other twentieth-century form of expression, has highlighted
that status so much as to make it "enough to question the cleavage between
the real and the imaginary."[124] From this perspective, the mutual precession of statements such as "it looks like a movie" and "it looks real" is
emblematic. Still in the same perspective, cinema made familiar to us
the paradoxical experience Merleau-Ponty describes apropos of painting
in *Eye and Mind*: "I would be hard pressed to say where the painting is
I am looking at. For I do not look at it as one looks at a thing, fixing it
in its place [. . .] Rather than seeing it, I see according to, or with it."[125]

Thus, if the image is not a "second thing," this is because of its
mutual precession with "what is." And it is precisely because of this mutual
precession that we see *according to, or with* images. Cinema has made
the links among these three Merleau-Pontian formulations manifest in our
experience, but we are just beginning to develop philosophy according to
their implications and consequences.

Chapter Five

The Light of the Flesh

Anti-Platonistic Instances and Neoplatonic Traces in the Later Merleau-Ponty's Thinking

> I love today's art because I love Light above all else
>
> —Guillaume Apollinaire

"A New Idea of Light"

The analysis above led me to highlight that, in the reflections Merleau-Ponty consecrated to cinema, the programmatic attention toward appearing—after which phenomenology itself is named—conjugates and feeds with the overriding consideration of the whole, which makes the Gestalt-theorie affirm the indecomposable feature of the perceived phenomena. On the one hand, this addresses such reflections toward a notion of perception as montage operating according to the peculiar logic binding our body to the world. On the other hand, this implies some increasingly profound critiques against metaphysics meant as a thinking that places, on the contrary, the true beyond appearing itself. Such critiques led Merleau-Ponty's later thinking to try to no longer conceive the giving of the true by following the traditional opposition—built by Plato in the Allegory of the Cave—between the deceiving shadows of what appears and the pure light emanating from truth. The giving of the true shall rather be conceived on the basis of an essential complementarity between light and shade.

63

Among the constants crossing the last courses Merleau-Ponty gave at the Collège de France, one can indeed find the search for what he defines—in the preparatory notes for the course titled "Philosophy and Non-Philosophy since Hegel"—as "a new idea of light." On this subject, he explains, "truth is of itself *zweideutig* [. . .]. The *Vieldeutigkeit* is not a shadow to be eliminated from true light."[1]

Evidently, this cannot but suggest an *ontological rehabilitation of the surface on which appearing shows itself.* Such a surface shall no longer be thought as a *veil* that would conceal the true and that shall hence be removed or even pierced. Rather, it shall be considered as a *screen* that reveals itself to be the decisive condition to *make seen* the images in which truth is manifested—just like in the case of the figure-ground relation or in the perception of the stroboscopic movement.[2] Such a rehabilitation may thus be characterized as the progressive affirmation of a different way of conceiving the giving of the true, which, from a *theatrical* configuration—namely, a *representative* configuration par excellence, opening at the opening of the curtain—gets to a *cinematic* configuration.

In short: the ontological rehabilitation of the surface, which leads us to consider the screen as the condition of possibility of vision, is one and the same with "a new idea of light" as *inseparable* from shade, for it is indeed the ground of the screen that *makes visible* the truth of the shared mutual appearing of shade and light.

Among the authors Merleau-Ponty confronts on this issue in his last courses are not only Hegel and Nietzsche,[3] but also Schelling (about whom I shall talk mainly by referring to the brilliant interpretation by an eminent Italian specialist of his reflection, that is, Francesco Moiso),[4] Descartes (whom my analysis will not directly evoke), and Proust, on whom I shall focus first of all. In addition to such references, another one, recurrent in Merleau-Ponty's last texts and notes, shall be flagged. Namely, a passage from Hermes Trismegistus, taken from an important article written in 1912 by the painter Robert Delaunay (and translated in German by Paul Klee),[5] to which Merleau-Ponty explicitly refers only in *Eye and Mind.*

Delaunay's article, significantly titled "Light," comes to the conclusion that "painting is in fact a luminous language," just after quoting this hermetic passage from the *Poimandres*: "*Soon the shadows will descend* [. . .] *and from them came an inarticulate cry which seemed to be the Voice of light.*"[6]

In *Eye and Mind* Merleau-Ponty confirms that: "art [. . .] is truly the 'inarticulate cry,' as Hermes Trismegistus said, 'which seemed to be the voice of the light.' And once it is present it awakens powers dormant in ordinary vision, a secret of preexistence. [. . .] This inner animation, this radiation of the visible, is what the painter seeks beneath the words *depth, space* and *color.*"[7]

The echo of Hermes Trismegistus's passage recurs twice in the preparatory notes of Merleau-Ponty's other course that was interrupted, just like "Philosophy and Non-Philosophy since Hegel," by his sudden death. We already know that the notes for this other course—which I mentioned in the chapter 4 of this book, and whose title is "Cartesian Ontology and the Ontology of Today"—see contemporary art and literature converge in the expression of an ontological mutation whose features they seem to better specify.

It is precisely within this fundamental consideration that the characterization of painting proposed by Delaunay is evoked by a first quote involving Hermes Trismegistus's terms. Such terms allow us to describe the painter's work through the reversibility between seeing and being seen, which—according to Merleau-Ponty—those terms exemplarily present by avoiding any distinction between activity and passivity. Precisely in this indistinction, the reflexivity of Being—in a Neoplatonic language, the reflexivity of "light"—seems to express itself, or indeed assume a "voice." In short, such terms evade the subject-object face-to-face imposed by the Cartesian ontology. Indeed, the second time Merleau-Ponty recalls Hermes Trismegistus's terms, he opposes them to those of Descartes in a concise note: "'Natural light' and 'cry of the light.'"[8]

The terms describing contemporary literature in the notes of the same course are similar. As I already mentioned, Merleau-Ponty lingers particularly on Proust's work, especially on the pages where he believes he is coming across a conception of ideas on which he comments as follows: "One says platonism, but these ideas are without an intelligible sun, and are akin to the visible light."[9] Therefore, it is no surprise to see that the Proustian pages in which Merleau-Ponty finds the trace of "a new idea of light" are precisely those that seem to sketch an anti-Platonistic theory of ideas. What may seem surprising is rather the convergence Merleau-Ponty suggests between these traces and the passage taken from a text, crucial for Neoplatonism, like the *Poimandres.*

"Ideas Without an Intelligible Sun": Proust

We have already come across the Proustian pages Merleau-Ponty comments on, since he never ceases referring to them all through his reflections. In such pages from the first volume of the Recherche, Proust distinguishes the "musical ideas"—but also the literary ideas, and "the notions of light, of sound, of perspective, of bodily desire, the rich possession wherewith our inner temple is diversified and adorned"—from the "ideas of the intelligence." In fact, the former are above all characterized as being "veiled in shadows" and hence "impenetrable by the human mind, which none the less were perfectly distinct one from another, unequal among themselves in value and in significance."[10]

Insofar as they examine once more the same Proustian pages on which Merleau-Ponty was commenting by the time of his death in the manuscript of *The Visible and the Invisible*, the preparatory notes I am considering here acquire an increased matter of interest, suggesting the possible developments of such a commentary.[11]

As we know, Merleau-Ponty's commentary already defined as "sensible" the ideas described by Proust,[12] since they are inseparable from their sensible presentation. Consequently, on the one hand, they appear as offered to our sensible finitude, and on the other hand, differently from "the ideas of the intelligence," they reveal their impossibility to be isolated as positive beings, and to be actively graspable. This is why Merleau-Ponty interprets this Proustian characterization in an essentially anti-Platonistic sense.

As for the course notes, they consider the reasons for which such ideas are assimilated by Proust, in particular,[13] to light. More precisely, to the "visible light," as we have seen, and not to the light of the Cartesian *intuitus mentis*.[14] In fact, Proust writes: "so long as we are alive, we can no more bring ourselves to a state in which we shall not have known them than we can with regard to any material object, then we can, for example, doubt the luminosity of a lamp that has just been lighted, in view of the changed aspect of everything in the room, from which has vanished even the memory of the darkness."[15]

Merleau-Ponty remarks: "Light is not a *quale*, it is the impossibility of *darkness*, [. . .] luminosity is a structure of being [*être*]: Eternity of light while it is [*pendant qu'elle est*]."[16] Similarly to the encounter with light, the encounter with ideas such as "the conception of love and happiness" radiated by the Vinteuil Sonata is thus, as Merleau-Ponty explains, "initiation to a *world*, to a small eternity, to a dimension, by now inalienable—Universality through singularity."[17] If then "the notions of the visible resemble to the musical ideas," as Merleau-Ponty observes, it is because both are "presences by radiation."[18] In fact, he continues, "here as there, in light as well as in [the] musical idea, we have an idea that is not *what* we see, but is behind it."[19] Where such a transcendence prevents us from taking possession of such ideas—that is, from *conceptually grasping them*, since, just like the light, they are ungraspable—this very transcendence obliges them for its part to show themselves precisely in what they illuminate— again, just like the light. This is what happens to a particular idea of love through the listening to the music that, in a certain time, had been the "national anthem" of the love between Swann and Odette.

In this sense, Merleau-Ponty makes a remark referring to the lines in which Proust writes that the notions of "light, of sound, of perspective, of bodily desire" are "the rich possession wherewith our inner temple is diversified and adorned." That is to say, wherewith "that great black impenetrable night, discouraging exploration, of our soul, which we have been content to regard as valueless and waste and void," is adorned. Here is Merleau-Ponty's remark: "Hence, nocturne reality of the soul, of incorpo- real things—which is not nothingness—, but needs to be 'adorned' with the visible—which is like [the] reverse of the visible."[20] In short, this "reality" needs—as Proust, again, writes—to espouse "our mortal state," it needs to be inscribed in our experience revealing itself as its "key feature or double," in order to show itself at least in the "oneirism (dream) of the sensible."[21] The inalienability of the sensible idea with respect to our life will hence constitute what Merleau-Ponty calls a "small eternity," evoking once more the indestructible characteristic of the mythical time, which I questioned in the last paragraph of the previous chapter.

Besides, although here Merleau-Ponty interprets the relation between the sensible and the ideal by resorting to the crucial reference of the light example, this interpretation shows a decisive distance with respect to the Neoplatonic framework. Indeed, such a framework characterizes light not as *visible*, but as *metaphysical*. In fact, Neoplatonism celebrates the sen- sible only insofar as it does not cease to refer to a superior *otherness*, thus opening to humanity—as we saw Panofsky highlight concerning Plotinus in the second chapter of the present work—"the prospect of the world of Ideas but at the same time *veiling* the view."[22]

In Merleau-Ponty's conception—as well as in the quote from Nietzsche he translates, which I recalled at the beginning of this chapter[23]—the question of the "veil" of the sensible is radically transformed. Actually, instead of *concealing* ideas, such a veil—of which light is, significantly, an essential component—*makes them visible*, revealing itself to be the very possibility of their radiation. Hence, what is the convergence suggested by Merleau-Ponty all about—namely, the convergence between the traces of "a new idea of light" and the characterization of light exposed in Hermes Trismegistus's sentence?

In order to answer this question, a reference shall be made to the fourth occurrence of this sentence in a passage from one of Merleau-Ponty's last writings. Such a passage is part of the "Draft for a Writing" of the chapter "Interrogation and Intuition" of *The Visible and the Invisible*, dated October 1960, which was to be replaced by a further version and eventually published along with the notes of Merleau-Ponty's last courses "on the possibility of philosophy today." The pages in which this passage appears also concern this question. Their main aim is to refuse philosophy's recurrent tendency to consider "language as a screen between [philosophy] itself and Being."[24] Merleau-Ponty opposes to such a tendency the fact that speech, even the philosophical speech, is prefigured in our sensible experience by the auto-organization of a "tacit sense."[25] Such a sense is what he defined already in *Phenomenology of Perception*—with Husserl—as "logos of the aesthetic world." Or what—in a working note of *The Visible and the Invisible*, which I previously mentioned—he qualifies, resorting to a totally different tradition, as "the λόγος ἐνδιάθετος [implicit *logos*] which calls for the λόγος προφορικός [spoken *logos*]."[26] It is precisely what he assimilates, in the passage examined here, to "what Hermes Trismegistus calls 'the cry of the light.'"[27]

Hence, if the "screen" of language Merleau-Ponty talks about does not present that insurmountable obstacle to the contemplation of Being that we often believed it coincided with, but rather offers itself to philosophy so as to show the sketch of a "spoken logos," this is because what gets articulated in it is solicited and even *invoked* by the "cry" of a sense which, for its part, *shines its own light* on another screen, on another veil. Such is the veil of the sensible, which, rather than concealing in a Platonistic way, eventually reveals itself to be a possibility of *making visible*.

The Diffused Lighting of Logos: Schelling

Such a framework explains why—as Moiso points out in the intervention I mentioned in the beginning—"Merleau-Ponty indicates that the most interesting moment of Schelling's *Naturphilosophie* is precisely the conception of light."[28] In fact, Moiso shows how Merleau-Ponty rightly recognizes in this conception the idea of a "diffused reason"[29] in Nature, which can thus indeed pre-tend [*pré-tendre*] to the "saying-collecting" that is involved in the Greek notion of logos.[30] This is why Merleau-Ponty recalls, quoting Jasper's book,[31] how Schelling disapproves that "[l]ight is only a medium in Fichte, so it is in 'no way the symbol of primordial and eternal knowing [*Urwissen*] which is incorporated [*eingebildet*] in Nature.' "[32]

Merleau-Ponty thus thinks that the conception according to which "luminosity is a structure of being [*être*]" is shared by Schelling, so much that the former lends the latter his own terminology when he alerts us to the fact that "to refuse this [. . .] meaning of Being is to make every carnal relation with Nature disappear."[33] In fact, only if the lighting is *structurally diffused* in the Being to which we belong (and thus maintains its *essential connection with shade*), can it collect its rays in a *hub* of sense, which, however, is not "altogether itself without the human being who achieves this meaning,"[34] as Merleau-Ponty specifies.

In other words, it is only by being *already diffused in the flesh* of which we are ourselves interweaved, that through us such luminosity shall *concentrate* in the hub of a sense, without having to invoke the external intervention of a metaphysical or subjectivist principle (the latter being but a variant of the former).

Hence, in Merleau-Ponty's commentary on Schelling some lines appear, signaling—as Moiso highlights—"an important point of the Merleau-Pontian reflection that follows nearly faithfully Shelling's thought."[35] Here they are: "light may be considered as matter, but light is also something other: it is subtle, it penetrates everywhere, explores the field promoted by our gaze and prepares it to be read. Light is a sort of concept that walks among appearances; it does not have a subjective existence, save when it becomes for us. Light does not know the world, but I see the world thanks to light."[36]

Moiso comments on this as follows: "Hence, light is a knowledge, for the knowledge of the world cannot be out of light. But at the same time, this knowledge is simply the possibility of seeing the world thanks to it [. . .] in the sense in which Schelling referred in 1804 to a diffused reason, meant as a preparatory knowledge which would not be knowledge yet, but which would be at the same time the fundament of knowledge."[37]

Darkness and the Voice of Light: Hermes Trismegistus (Flesh as *Khôra*)

Knowing all this, let us go back to Hermes Trismegistus's sentence. Or rather, to the pages of *Poimandres*, the writing from which the passage Delaunay commented on—the one recalled by Merleau-Ponty—is extracted. Besides, it is important to point out that Merleau-Ponty always quotes this passage in the terms of Delaunay's article, rather than directly resorting to the writing's French translation, which was then already at our disposal in the philologically accredited version published by André-Jean Festugière in 1945.[38]

The *Poimandres* pages from which this sentence is extracted are the first ones. Here, one can read how *Poimandres* offers to the meditating believer the following revealing vision: "and in an instant everything was immediately opened to me. I saw an endless vision in which everything became light—clear and joyful—and in seeing the vision I came to love it. After a little while, darkness arose separately and descended—fearful and gloomy—coiling sinuously so that it looked to me like a [snake]. Then the darkness changed into something of a watery nature, indescribably agitated and smoking like a fire; it produced an unspeakable wailing roar. Then an inarticulate cry like the voice of fire came forth from it. But from the light . . . a holy word mounted upon the [watery] nature, and untempered fire leapt up from the watery nature to the height above."[39]

It is evident that we are here in front of a cosmological vision recalling the mythical reconstruction of the cosmic demiurgy exposed by Plato in the *Timaeus*. Such a reconstruction, as is well known, broadens by considering first two, and then three components in the second part of Timaeus's discourse: "For the purpose of what we have hitherto said, it was enough to distinguish between two things, our postulated intelligible and perpetually self-same model in the first place and its transient visible copy in the second. In our original distinction we introduced no further third term, as we supposed that these two would suffice us; now, it seems, our discourse compels us to attempt the exposition of a perplexed and obscure concept. What quality and nature, then, must we ascribe to it? Something of this kind: that it is the receptacle, the foster-mother [τιθήνην] as I might say, of all becoming."[40]

The third term or "component" introduced here is thus the *khôra*, which Plato connects to the other two resorting to a genealogical myth. His reconstruction thus disposes us to think of the cosmogonic question in terms of filiation: "for the present, meanwhile, we must conceive three terms, that which becomes, that wherein it becomes, that on the model whereof that which becomes comes to be. We may further properly compare the recipient with a mother, the model with a father, that which arises between them with their child, and may reflect that there is to be a casting exhibiting all manner of diversities, the vehicle wherein it is cast will not have been duly prepared unless it is devoid of all those forms it is to receive from elsewhere."[41]

In his turn, Poimandres recalls these terms of filiation in order to explain the revealing vision quoted before: "I am the light you saw, mind, your god [. . .] who existed before the watery nature that appeared out of darkness. The lightgiving word who comes from mind is the son of god."[42] Let us focus our attention on the characteristics that Plato assigns to this "watery nature that appeared out of darkness"—namely, the *khôra*—in this genealogical perspective of filiation:

> This, then, is why we are not to call the mother and receptacle of all creation visible and sensible generally earth, nor air, nor fire, nor water, nor any of their compounds nor constituents; but if we say it is a somewhat invisible [ἀνόρατον] and formless [ἄμορφον], all-receptive and partaking of the intelligible in a manner most puzzling and hard to grasp, we shall not be wrong. So far as its character may be discerned from what we have premised, the truest account of it would be as follows; that such part of it as is ignited appears from time to time as fire, such as is liquefied as water, or as earth and air, so far as it receives copies [μιμήματα] of them.[43]

Hence, according to such a genealogical perspective, the Platonic *khôra* reveals itself to be a "third component" characterized as a matrix, receiving from the first one—that of the immutable models, namely, the ideas—the *images* (μιμήματα) whose sensible copies it generates.

In the *Poimandres* sentence quoted by Delaunay, however, Merleau-Ponty seems to find the description of a "*component*" that is not informed by an external model, but is *at once amorphous and informative*[44] of itself, since its very darkness seems to emanate that "inarticulate cry like the voice of light." This "component" is thus at once amorphous darkness and structural luminosity, which, in propagating itself, differentiates both the living and nonliving beings. In other words, it confers on them an individual identity, and yet does not cut them out of the darkness of what we can call—with reference to an expression by Anaxagoras often quoted by Merleau-Ponty—their "being together,"[45] that is, their being intertwined in the same flesh. It is precisely a similar ontological principle (not "third," but rather *unitary texture of differences in constant differentiation*) that Merleau-Ponty tried to elaborate by the name "flesh," or—as we saw apropos

of Schelling—by the name of "Nature." Regarding Nature, it is not by
chance that in a working note of *The Visible and the Invisible* he indeed
affirms that "it is the flesh, the mother."[46]

Hence, what Merleau-Ponty tried to elaborate reveals itself to be a
sort of *khôra* that is not formed *in the light* of the exterior, prior models.
In fact, it is in this very *khôra* that are differentiated—and thus *come to
light*—those images which, resonating with one another, shall possibly
sediment in models. Such models will therefore end up being *produced
models* which, in their turn, shall however remain secretly *inseparable* from
those images, as the "sensible ideas" described by Proust teach us. As
we already know, to describe ideas as inseparable from the flesh in which
they manifest themselves—should it be the "veil" of the sensible or the
"screen" of words—is to describe the rays of a light that *shows itself only
in the very filigree that it shows*. Light *of the* flesh, hence, in the double
meaning of this genitive: namely, of course, light that can illuminate the
flesh, but only insofar as it is diffused by the flesh itself. This is the very
light that, in the sentence quoted by Delaunay, Hermes Trismegistrus seems
to assimilate to the cry emanating *from darkness itself*.

For Merleau-Ponty, the flesh is hence a condition of possibility insofar
as it is a condition of visibility by difference: in this consists its structural
luminosity. To be visible thus means to arrest this luminosity tracing the
individual outlines, and *with them*, their shadow. As a consequence, such
a shadow would not be deceiving, *false*, unless it were separated from the
luminosity that produced it. In other words: unless one pretended that such
a luminosity *is not essentially* bound to that shadow.

Moreover, if we recall the Neoplatonist features attributing to God
a creative imagination, we can think of that kind of *khôra* Merleau-Ponty
tried to elaborate as the condition of possibility of creation—a creation
remaining in any case left to *us*, as we read in Schelling's commentary—of
the images, whose memory it will later welcome in the *form* of *models*.

Many of the elements unfolding here find a mutual clarification in
a most dense working note of *The Visible and the Invisible*, to which I
already referred before, and in which one of the decisive issues Plato
attributes to the *khôra* is significantly evoked. Let us read this note as a
conclusion: "The 'amorphous' perceptual world that I spoke of in relation
to painting—perceptual resources for the remaking of painting—which
contains no mode of expression and which nonetheless calls them forth
and requires all of them and which arouses again with each painter a
new effort of expression—this perceptual world is at bottom Being in Heidegger's sense, which is more than all painting, more than all speech, than

every 'attitude,' and which, apprehended by philosophy in its universality, appears as containing everything that will ever be said, and yet leaving us to create it (Proust): it is the λόγος ἐνδιάθετος [implicit *logos*] which calls for the λόγος προφορικός [spoken *logos*]."[47]

Chapter Six

The Sensible Ideas Between
Life and Philosophy

"A-Philosophy"

As we know, in *Eye and Mind*, Merleau-Ponty remarks that modern paintings give him the impression that in our age the relationship of humans
to themselves, to others, to things, and to the world—namely, the knot of
relations that to him constitutes what we call Being—does not manifest
itself in the same way that it did in the past.[1]

Why does Merleau-Ponty claim this while referring to painting?
Because painting in the twentieth century has openly rejected all mimetic
hypotheses. This is witnessed, for instance, by Paul Klee's famous declaration that "art does not reproduce the visible; it makes visible." To reject
all mimetic hypotheses means in turn to reject the ideas that the world is
a spectacle unfurling before my eyes, that painting would be called upon
to *represent* it on a canvas conceived as a window or a mirror, and that
the image would be nothing but a "second thing." Consequently, rejecting
the mimetic hypothesis means implicitly calling into question those concepts traditionally describing our relation to Being, such as the *opposition*
between subject and object, which is supposed to designate what is *in
front of* us. In this traditional perspective, the world appears as the "great
object" in which I am not implicated myself: it constitutes the spectacle I
am supposed to represent, either pictorially on the canvas, or conceptually
in thought. This is why, in *Eye and* Mind, Merleau-Ponty writes that every
theory of painting is a metaphysics,[2] meaning that every theory of painting
implies the idea of a certain relationship to Being.

But for Merleau-Ponty, the reference to painting is not the only one that testifies to the mutation at work in the relations between humans and Being. Indeed, in those very years, by explaining how science, or rather *the sciences* of the twentieth century, have modified our conception of nature, he claims that this mutation in the scientific conception of nature is in turn the sign of an overall ontological mutation, which must be definitely encouraged, since it is absolutely necessary.[3] For him, this mutation is a matter of an ongoing process, which at the same time must be developed.

Merleau-Ponty thus sees this process of mutation at work in very different domains—painting and the physical and biological sciences, for example—but in nevertheless convergent directions. As we have seen, this leads him to speak of a "fundamental thought,"[4] which he says has not yet found the means to realize itself as an explicit philosophy—that is, it has not yet found the attitude and language to express itself in what the Western tradition calls precisely "philosophy."

We see then that the direction and goal of Merleau-Ponty's later thought oblige us to pose the very questions to which I have just alluded: if—from the natural sciences, on the one hand, and pictorial experience, on the other hand (but also from cinematic, literary, and musical experiences)—a new pattern of relations between humans and Being emerges, will the idea of philosophy formulated by the Western tradition still be able to take up the attitude and the language *to speak of* this mutation? Or will it instead be necessary to rethink the very idea of philosophy? And, if this is the case, then what mutations in the idea of philosophy will be necessary to speak of the mutations of the relations between human and Being? Are these indispensable mutations in the very idea of philosophy even possible? That is, even if we should succeed in imprinting these changes in our thought, will they still allow us to speak of philosophy as we have until now?

To try to answer these questions, Merleau-Ponty, in his last course at the Collège de France, interrogated, on the one hand, *a certain* philosophical tradition, one to which he felt he belonged, one that could not avoid taking the thought of Descartes as a problematically fundamental point of reference and that had as other, no less fundamental points of reference the most important thinkers of the phenomenological movement, namely, Husserl and Heidegger. On the other hand, Merleau-Ponty also began to look for additional references to deal with what he called, by a peculiar expression, the "history of a-philosophy."[5]

By this expression, Merleau-Ponty wanted to point to a lineage—begun, according to him, by Hegel and continued by Marx, Kierkegaard, and Nietzsche, then by Husserl and Heidegger—whose different attempts at thought wanted, each in his own way, to go beyond simply raising different theoretical options, and instead to take sides with those areas of experience that philosophy, as it has traditionally been constituted, forced out of its field of research—attempts at thought that have aimed to take sides with "nonphilosophy." To advocate the reasons of appearing *along with* those of Being, as Hegel did with the fundamental principles of his phenomenology of spirit, to advocate the reasons of experience rather than those of abstract thought, to advocate the demands of life rather than those of theory (as, for example, in Nietzsche's *Zarathustra*: "I beseech you my brothers, remain faithful to the earth"),[6] to advocate the reasons of "this side" rather than the metaphysical "beyond"—these are all, thinks Merleau-Ponty, the many attempts to consider the reasons of nonphilosophy against the traditional identity with which philosophy had provided itself.

When Merleau-Ponty speaks of "a-philosophy," he wants to indicate a thought that knows how to make the reasons of the *nonphilosophical* its own, and thanks to them is also able to radically transform the identity of the *philosophical*. As Merleau-Ponty puts it in one of the notes that can be found in the beginning of his course titled Philosophy and Non-Philosophy since Hegel, to which I am referring, it is a "philosophy wanting to be philosophy while remaining non-philosophy [. . .], [that] has access to the absolute, not as 'beyond,' as a positive second-order, but as another order which must be on this side, the double-inaccessible without being passed through—real philosophy makes fun of philosophy, it is a-philosophy."[7]

These words allow us to judge the full scope of the task with which Merleau-Ponty took himself to be involved. But his sudden death at the age of fifty-three interrupted his research; we are left only with some elements that are absolutely insufficient to restore unequivocally the signs of a thought equal to the stakes that such research had set for itself. They are instead the elements in which thought *seeks itself* by confronting the twentieth-century sciences of nature, contemporary pictorial, literary or musical experiences, and certain currents of the philosophical tradition. So, as Merleau-Ponty wrote, referring to Husserl, it is a thought that circumscribes "a domain yet to be thought,"[8] a domain defined by questions or interrogations to which we can remain faithful and that we can find again "only by thinking once again."[9]

Several cultural symptoms thus converge, according to Merleau-Ponty, on the expression of a new relationship between humans and Being, and we know that Marcel Proust and his *In Search of Lost Time* occupy a central place in this panorama, as Merleau-Ponty describes in *The Visible and the Invisible*: "No one has gone further than Proust in fixing the relations between the visible and the invisible, in describing an idea that is not the contrary of the sensible, that is its lining and its depth."[10] In the last years of Merleau-Ponty's life, characterized by the research to which I am referring, the crucial reason why he turns to Proust is that pointed out in the above-quoted sentence. Indeed, it emphasizes once more that an appropriate philosophical formulation of our new relationship to Being passes through a new description of the relationship between the sensible and the intelligible—namely, it passes through a non-Platonist theory of ideas, and hence of images, to which, for Merleau-Ponty, Proust more than anyone has come closest.

It is clear that a theory of ideas can only imply a theory of their genesis, or a theory of ideation, which in turn is inseparable from a new conception of the relation between activity and passivity; whose distinction traditionally characterizes the "place" where we usually say ideas *happen*: this place that we call "subject." In approaching this topic, however, I must explicitly assume responsibility for thinking through the shreds of reflection passed down by Merleau-Ponty.[11]

The Simultaneous Genesis of an Idea and a Hollow

With that said, in order to understand how a theory of ideation, of the genesis of ideas, may—somehow consequently—arise from the non-Platonist intent that Merleau-Ponty locates in Proust, I propose to begin with a sentence from Merleau-Ponty himself and to try to understand what consequences can be drawn from it. Here is the sentence: "When we invent a melody, the melody sings in us more than we sing it, it goes down into the throat of the singer, as Proust says [. . .] [T]he body is suspended in what it sings: the melody is incarnated and finds in the body a type of servant."[12]

Is it possible to say that we are faced here with a description of the genesis of an idea? I would say yes. We find a description of the genesis of a musical idea known as "melody." Now, as we have understood, when we invent a melody, it "sings in us more than we sing it." Ideation thus consists of an attitude, which elsewhere Merleau-Ponty, following Heidegger, spoke about in terms of a "letting be" [*sein lassen*]. Indeed, if it is true that, when we invent a melody, it "sings in us much more than we sing it," then we can say that inventing is a *letting-be*, which in turn consists—as Merleau-Ponty suggested at the same time—in giving the world and things "the *resonance* they demand."[13]

Let us return now to the preceding citation: "When we invent a melody, the melody sings in us more than we sing in it: it goes down the throat of the singer." We could say that "inventing" understood as "letting-be" consists, in other words, of a *welcoming* matching with a process of *according oneself* with the encounter of the world, in a triple manner that nonetheless has an intimately unitary meaning: to let the encounter with the world be by letting *oneself* be in the encounter, by the entry into resonance with it. This is in fact how the singer welcomes in his throat the melody that descends into it and is sung in him. But if this is all true, how can we who characterize ourselves as inventing a melody by welcoming it define ourselves? We can say that we are the *hollows* that welcome the melody and the birth of such an idea.

Obviously, it would be wrong to understand our being-hollow in the sense of being a pure and simple "receptacle" of the idea, to echo the word by which, as we know, Plato characterized the *khôra*.[14] It would be wrong for at least two reasons. First, it would imply thinking of this hollow as already existing *before* the idea happens, and thus thinking of it precisely as a hollow that is content to shelter such an idea. In other words, it would imply thinking of ourselves in terms of a *pure passivity*. Moreover, to reduce ourselves to a pure and simple receptacle, always ready to shelter any idea that might happen, would suggest that *this idea preexisted as such "elsewhere"* and that it would have one day decided to fall into the also already preconstituted hollow that we are.

We have seen that we should instead understand the description of the genesis of the idea, as well as the genesis of the hollow—which we can no longer strictly speaking call a "subject"—as the description of *two aspects of the same event*, which we can characterize as *putting into reciprocal resonance*. An event that consists precisely in the *simultaneous* advent of the idea and of our being-hollow. We do not therefore have to seek to know whether this event occurs within us *or* exterior to us, since it is *both* interior and exterior at once, produced in the encounter and *as* the encounter of interiority and exteriority. Such an encounter, as an event, is inevitably clarified by the light of a *shock*. It produces itself as the encounter that crosses the texture of differences joining us to the world—that is, the texture Merleau-Ponty calls "flesh"—making that texture resonate, as Deleuze might specify, by the *effects* of resemblance,[15] or even identity, which in this case we shall call "ideas." Simultaneously, the encounter event produces a sort of "invagination, or padding"[16]—the term is significantly both Merleau-Ponty's and Deleuze's[17]—of a piece of the very texture of flesh, folding it back into a resonating hollow that welcomes and sediments the idea that *happened* in the encounter.

Thus, neither does the hollow exist prior to the idea, nor the idea prior to the hollow; rather, both my becoming-hollow where the melody resonates, *and* the formation of the melody through that resonance, happen *together*. To put it in the words of the French poet Paul Claudel, they are "*co-born*."[18] More exactly, they are born together *in an indistinction of activity and passivity*. In fact, Merleau-Ponty's sentence that interests us here is like the Möbius strip I evoked in the chapter 4: there is an active sense that is implicitly doubled by a passive sense that stays exactly *the same*. Thus, both senses together speak of a reflexive sense in which activity and passivity appear indistinct, and thereby the distinction between a supposedly acting subject and an acted-on object is lost. Indeed, Merleau-Ponty writes: "When we invent a melody" (here, "we" is subject and the verbal form is active), "the melody is sung in us" (here "we" lose the position of subject and the verbal form simultaneously becomes reflexive). In a working note of *The Visible and the Invisible*, Merleau-Ponty emphasizes precisely this while speaking specifically of the *hollow* [*creux*] to characterize what I have just tried to describe. He writes that thinking is not "an *activity* of the soul, nor a production of thoughts in the plural, and I am not even the author of that *hollow* that forms within me by the passage from the present to retention, it is not I who makes myself think any more than it is I who makes my heart beat."[19]

Hence, although I am not the author of my thoughts or of this hollow that forms within me, something creates *itself* in the hollow—or better, *with* it: a melody, for example. It is like saying that a process of creation is triggered in me without me being its author. Or that "welcoming," which is traditionally supposed to signify a passive attitude, and "creating," which is traditionally supposed to mean an active attitude, *are one and the same*. And it also means that the idea does not exist prior to its advent, which is another decisively anti-Platonist element.

I would like to emphasize how what I have so far tried to describe shows that *an idea* thus *happens in our encounter with the world* and within a wider horizon of relations that we call Being. In this sense, the advent of an idea shows itself from then on as an *ontological event* rather than as our own private "mental event." But we shall also emphasize how the process I have been trying to describe so far, by which a hollow opens within us and because of which something is created in that opening of the hollow, applies not only to the advent of ideas, but also to the advent of values. In fact, those values that underlie our actions also seem to be forming within us by virtue of the creative passivity of which I am speaking.[20]

Whether it is a question of ideas or values, we have seen how they are created in our becoming-hollow. In this sense, we are not their authors, because it is not we who shape them, but rather *our meeting with the world*, which, as Merleau-Ponty wrote in his later lecture notes on nature, gives them expression in a thought that works "without thinking,"[21] that is, in a still *blind* thought, or, as Proust would say, in a thought whose ideas are "veiled in shadows." On the one hand, then, when we open ourselves as a hollow, an indistinction between our active and passive beings appears. On the other hand, what comes to be expressed in this indistinction is not shaped by ourselves but rather by the very being of our encounter with the world. It is this being that *is reflected* or, to put it in another way, that *is thought in us*. That is why I have said that the ideas that this way come to light are not mere "mental events," but rather ontological events.

Perhaps we have managed to make a little clearer some aspects of the mutating relationship between humans and Being that Merleau-Ponty saw at work in our age. Obviously this mutation does not consist in *inaugurating* the production of those dynamics that I have sought to make evident, as if now the ideas are born thus, while they once used to be born otherwise. The mutation lies rather in the fact that our age seems to be *bringing into expression* these experiences *in new ways*, thus producing what Deleuze defined in turn as the "profound elements for a new image of thought."[22] He reaffirms this a little further: "Yes, a new image of the act of thinking, of the way thought operates, of its genesis in thought itself, that is what we are looking for."[23]

Thus, this age would have brought (or rather—with reference to the Latin etymology of the word *concept* I evoked in the third chapter—brought back) to expression our being-hollow, which is neither being a void nor a plenitude, even though the philosophical tradition has privileged an idea of the subject according to one or the other of these two models—that is, according to the tradition, the subject is either a plenitude that gives meaning to the world, or a void that receives meaning from the world.

To bring the mutation of the relations between humans and Being to expression therefore means describing our being not as a "subject" that faces an "object-world," as I explained earlier, but rather as the "hollow" that is a "sounding board" in the sense that we have heard Merleau-Ponty speak of a melody that *is sung* in us, provided that we accord to it the resonance it requires. It is actually a hollow in which our encounter with the flesh of the world resonates, where that resonance is not the mere reproduction of a sound produced elsewhere, but rather—and this is what the sounding board teaches us—it takes on a particular creative value.

In the same perspective, perhaps we have not yet sufficiently emphasized that the characterization of our being in terms of "becoming-hollow," of "invagination," is complementary to the characterization of the idea's being that Merleau-Ponty draws from what Proust wrote of "musical motifs." Being, traditionally considered as what endures beyond the deceptive visibility of becoming but that is nevertheless accessible by another mode of *vision*—precisely, the being of an idea—here shows its ineffaceable sensible rootedness, and shows it first thanks to that art that is canonically related to time and thus to becoming, an art that offers itself as a mode of encounter—*listening*—that as such shields it from the paradigm of the face to face and from representation, an art that therefore allows us to think our being, as well as the being of the idea, in nonsubstantive, even nonidentifying terms: music, of course.[24]

I am approaching the conclusion. I tried to describe a relationship of indivision between activity and passivity, a relation that is one and the same as *a creativity that we are, yet without being its authors*. To define such a relation, the most appropriate words seem to me to be those Merleau-Ponty uses to describe one of the decisive ideas of his later reflection, that of the chiasm, according to which, he says, "every relation with being is *simultaneously* a taking and a being taken, the hold is held, it is *inscribed* and inscribed in the same being that it takes hold of."[25]

That should suffice to understand the meaning of those attempts at thought that according to Merleau-Ponty have followed from Hegel, and with which it seems obvious to me we are still involved. They are, as I explained at the beginning of this chapter, attempts that seek to formulate the present mutation of the relations between humans and Being in a thought that, in order to be expressed, must in its turn be transformed from philosophy into a-philosophy, at least according to the meaning and intent Merleau-Ponty gives to that term. In fact, if we are not subjects who confront the world, but rather hollows emerging as sounding boards from the encounter with the world, it is clear that this intention of "grasping" cannot exist and that it must be called into question. In this sense Merleau-Ponty writes that philosophy "is not *above* life, overhanging."[26] It is therefore not in a position to grasp life in order to have an intellectual possession of it.

Since Thales, however, philosophy has traditionally mistrusted life, it has always kept its distance from life, and it is precisely in this gesture of keeping distance from life that it has constituted its identity, considering life as nonphilosophy. Of course, I am referring here to the Platonic anecdote of Thales who, staring at the stars, fell into a pit while a Tracian maid mocked him.[27] A philosophy relating itself to nonphilosophy (and thus relating itself to life understood as one of the names that philosophy itself has attributed to nonphilosophy), by recognizing such nonphilosophy as the other side of its being philosophy rather than recognizing it as what is other than itself: this is precisely what the idea of philosophy that Merleau-Ponty defines as "a-philosophy" consists of. In such an idea, Merleau-Ponty sees the *principle* (in the double sense of an initial moment and a fundamental notion) in the Hegelian conception of phenomenology. Thus, when speaking of "a-philosophy," Merleau-Ponty writes: "according to Hegel, one attains the absolute by way of a phenomenology (the appearance of mind; mind in the phenomena). This is not because the phenomenal mind is on one level of a scale [. . .] but because the absolute would not be absolute if it did not appear as absolute."[28]

This means that appearing is a decisive and integral aspect of being, even though it traditionally represented only another name attributed by philosophy to what it considered to be nonphilosophy.

And so we have philosophy and nonphilosophy, just like sensible and intelligible, imaginary and real, activity and passivity, subject and object. The task that remains to be accomplished is to revoke the intention of opposition by which metaphysics has instituted all these dualisms (which can be summarized by the dualism of the visible and the invisible), in order instead to name the *intimate cobelonging* of their poles, and consequently to transform the attitude and language in a manner corresponding to the current mutation of the relations between humans and Being. Besides, it cannot be otherwise, since, beyond any singular biographies, it is not the task of a thinker, but that of thought itself.

Notes

Introduction

1. "It is this Visibility, this generality of the Sensible in itself, this anonymity innate to Myself that we have previously called flesh, and one knows there is no name in traditional philosophy to designate it" (M. Merleau-Ponty, *Le visible et l'invisible*, text established by C. Lefort [Paris: Gallimard, 1964]; trans. A. Lingis, *The Visible and the Invisible* [Evanston: Northwestern University Press, 1968], 139).

2. Ibid.

3. Ibid., 132.

4. Ibid., 149.

5. See ibid., 139, where such a sense is explained as follows: "not to see in the outside, as the others see it, the contour of a body one inhabits, but especially to be seen by the outside, to exist within it, to emigrate into it."

6. Ibid., 140.

7. See G. Deleuze, "Renverser le platonisme," in *Revue de Métaphysique et de Morale* 4, (1967), later republished as "Platon et le simulacre," in *Logique du sens* (Paris: Minuit, 1969); trans. M. Lester with C. Stivale, "Plato and the simulacrum," in *The Logic of Sense* (New York: Columbia University Press, 1990), 253–266.

8. M. Merleau-Ponty, *L'œil et l'esprit* [1960–61] (Paris: Gallimard, 1964); trans. M. B. Smith, "Eye and Mind," in ed. G. A. Johnson, *The Merleau-Ponty Aesthetics Reader* (Evanston: Northwestern University Press, 1993), 126.

9. For a discussion on this question from the standpoint of positions that are close to the ones I suggest here, see P. Rodrigo, *L'intentionnalité créatrice: Problèmes de phénoménologie et d'esthétique* (Paris: Vrin, 2009), 153–164; here 157.

10. M. Merleau-Ponty, *Signes* (Paris: Gallimard, 1960); trans. R. C. McCleary, *Signs* (Evanston: Northwestern University Press, 1964), 20–21.

11. This French word literally indicates "clairvoyance," but in view of the misunderstandings that might occur if the Platonistic meaning of such a notion were accepted, the original French term will be employed—Trans.

12. M. Merleau-Ponty, *Eye and Mind*, 132.

13. Henri Maldiney talks about an "originary *presence* according to an unobjective way of being" (H. Maldiney, "Le dévoilement de la dimension esthé-

tique dans la phénoménologie d'Erwin Straus" [1966], in *Regard Parole Espace* [Lausanne: L'Âge de l'Homme, 1994], 134).

14. M. Merleau-Ponty, *Eye and Mind*, 126.

15. M. Merleau-Ponty, *Notes de cours au Collège de France 1958–1959 et 1960–1961*, with a Preface by C. Lefort, text established by S. Ménasé (Paris: Gallimard, 1996), 173.

16. Ibid., my emphasis.

17. M. Merleau-Ponty, *Eye and Mind*, 126. See on this formulation not only the above quoted text by Rodrigo (above, note 9), but also that of J. Garelli titled "Voir ceci et voir selon," in eds. M. Richir and E. Tassin, *Merleau-Ponty: phénoménologie et experiences* (Grenoble: Millon, 1992), 79–99.

18. See G. Boehm, "Die Wiederkehr der Bilder," in ed. G. Boehm, *Was ist ein Bild?* (Munich: Fink, 1994), 11–38.

19. M. Merleau-Ponty, *The Visible and the Invisible*, 132.

20. Ibid., 132–133.

21. M. Merleau-Ponty, *Eye and Mind*, 139.

22. M. Merleau-Ponty, *The Visible and the Invisible*, 140.

23. G. Boehm "Ce qui montre. De la différence iconique," in ed. E. Alloa, *Penser l'image* (Dijon: Les presses du réel, 2010), 34. Before this, Boehm also writes that "As long as we will remain convinced [. . .] that what shows itself can also be said, images will have no strength" (ibid., 30).

24. Gottfried Boehm talks about an "iconic turn" referring to Merleau-Ponty (see ed. G. Boehm, *Was ist ein Bild?*, 21) right after explaining that "Merleau-Ponty also had to revise the phenomenological foundations of his thinking [. . .], wanting to achieve an adequate understanding of the eye and the image" (ibid., 30).

25. W. J. T. Mitchell, "What Do Pictures *Really* Want?," in ed. R. Krauss, *October* 77 (1996), 71–82.

26. Ibid., 72.

27. On this issue, see E. Escoubas, "La question de l'œuvre d'art: Merleau-Ponty et Heidegger," in eds. M. Richir and E. Tassin, *Merleau-Ponty: phénoménologie et expériences*, 123–128.

28. M. Merleau-Ponty, *Eye and Mind*, 47.

29. W. J. T. Mitchell, "What Do Pictures *Really* Want?," in *October* 77, 82.

30. G. Didi-Huberman, *Devant le temps: Histoire de l'art et anachronisme des images* (Paris: Minuit, 2000), 239.

31. "Essence and existence, imaginary and real, visible and invisible—painting scrambles all our categories, spreading out before us its oneiric universe of carnal essences, actualized resemblances, mute meanings" (M. Merleau-Ponty, *Eye and Mind*, p. 130).

Chapter One

1. See, for instance, §28 of E. Husserl, ed. W. Biemel, *Die Krisis der europäischen Wissenschaften und die transzendentale Phänomenologie* (Den Haag:

Martinus Nijhoff, 1954); trans. D. Carr, *The Crisis of European Sciences and Transcendental Phenomenology* (Evanston: Northwestern University Press, 1970).

2. M. Merleau-Ponty, *La Nature: Notes, Cours au Collège de France*, text established and with notes by D. Séglard (Paris: Seuil, 1995); trans. R. Vallier, *Nature: Course Notes from the Collège de France* (Evanston: Northwestern University Press, 2003), 4.

3. M. Merleau-Ponty, *The Visible and the Invisible*, 274.

4. Ibid., 147.

5. See ibid., 139, 145, and 147.

6. Ibid., 139–140 and 147.

7. Ibid., 217, as well as M. Merleau-Ponty, "Le philosophe et son ombre" [1959], in *Signs*; trans. "The Philosopher and His Shadow," p. 179. See also *Notes de cours au Collège de France 1958–1959 et 1960–1961*, 85.

8. M. Merleau-Ponty, *The Visible and the Invisible*, 124. One could interpret in a similar way the question of the "origin [*Ursprung*]" in the Benjaminian sense evoked by Didi-Huberman above. On this point, see in particular W. Benjamin, *Ursprung des deutschen Trauerspiels* (Berlin: Rowohlt, 1928); trans. J. Osborne, *The Origin of the German Tragic Drama* (London: Verso 2003).

9. See M. Merleau-Ponty, *The Visible and the Invisible*, and, even more clearly, the following passage from a working note to the same text: "for me it is no longer a question of *origins*, nor limits, nor of a series of events going to a first cause, but *one sole explosion of Being which is forever*" (ibid., 265, my emphasis).

10. M. Merleau-Ponty, "The Philosopher and His Shadow," in *Signs*, 167.

11. M. Merleau-Ponty, *The Visible and the Invisible*, 147.

12. E. Husserl, "Umsturz des kopernikanischen Lehre in der gewöhnlichen weltanschaulichen Interpretation. Die Ur-Arche bewegt sich nicht. Grundlegende Untersuchungen zum phänomenologischen Ursprung der Körperlichkeit, der Räumlichkeit der Natur im ersten naturwissenschaftlichen Sinne" [1934], in ed. M. Faber, *Philosophical Essays in Memory of Edmund Husserl* (Cambridge: Harvard University Press, 1940); trans. F. Kersten, "Foundational Investigations of the Phenomenological Origin of the Spatiality of Nature," in E. Husserl, eds. P. McCormick and F. A Elliston, *Shorter Works* (Notre Dame: University of Notre Dame Press and The Harvest Press, 1981), revised by L. Lawlor for inclusion in M. Merleau-Ponty, eds. L. Lawlor and B. Bergo, *Husserl at the Limits of Phenomenology* (Evanston: Northwestern University Press, 2002), 117–131. On this writing's influence on Merleau-Ponty's thought, see G. D. Neri, "Terra e Cielo in un manoscritto husserliano del 1934," in *aut aut*, N. 245, 1991, 40 ff.

13. M. Merleau-Ponty, *Résumés de cours. Collège de France 1952–1960* (Paris: Gallimard, 1968); trans. J. O'Neill, "Themes from the Lectures at the Collège de France, 1952–1960," in Merleau-Ponty, *In Praise of Philosophy and Other Essays* (Evanston: Northwestern University Press, 1988), 189. Translation modified.

14. Ibid., 190. Through this stone example Merleau-Ponty specifically refers to the following passage in Husserl's manuscript: "I can throw stones into the air and see them come back down as the same. The throwing can be more or less weak; obviously, the appearances are therefore analogous to motions based on the

earth so that they become experienced as motions" (E. Husserl, "Foundational Investigations of the Phenomenological Origin of the Spatiality of Nature," 124).

15. R. Delaunay, quoted in M. Merleau-Ponty, *Eye and Mind*, 146.

16. Husserl writes that the Earth "is the ark which makes possible in the first place the sense of all motion and all rest as modes of motion. But its rest is not a mode of motion" (E. Husserl, "Foundational Investigations of the Phenomenological Origin of the Spatiality of Nature," 130).

17. M. Merleau-Ponty, *Eye and Mind*, 142.

18. In this working note, Merleau-Ponty goes further: "The idea of chiasm and *Ineinander* is on the contrary the idea that every analysis that *disentangles* renders unintelligible [. . .]. It is a question of creating a new type of intelligibility (intelligibility through the world and Being as they are—'vertical' and not *horizontal*)" (M. Merleau-Ponty, *The Visible and the Invisible*, 268).

19. See D. Franck, *Chair et corps. Sur la phénoménologie de Husserl* (Paris: Minuit, 1981); trans. J. Riviera and S. Davidson, *Flesh and Body: On the Phenomenology of Husserl* (London-New York: Bloomsbury Academic, 2014). Franck is the French translator of Husserl's "Umsturz des kopernikanischen Lehre." Commenting on that text he wrote: "Husserl prepares here—and this is probably the greatest interest in this fragment—a conception of space and flesh eluding all physics and all geometry." (D. Franck, note on E. Husserl, "Umsturz des kopernikanischen Lehre," French trans. D. Franck, "L'arche-originaire de la Terre ne se meut pas," in *Philosophie* 1 (January 1984), 3). It shall also be pointed out that Bernhard Waldenfels translates in his turn Merleau-Ponty's term *chair* by the German *Leib*. See B. Waldenfels, *Phänomenologie in Frankreich* (Frankfurt am Main: Suhrkamp, 1983), 200. On this same point, see also G. Boehm, "Der stumme Logos," in eds. A. Métraux, B. Waldenfels, *Leibhaftige Vernunft, Spuren von Merleau-Pontys Denken* (Munich: Wilhelm Fink, 1986), 289–304.

20. Such is the title of the last chapter of Franck's book *Heidegger et le problème de l'espace* (Paris: Minuit, 1986).

21. The Husserlian notion of *Leib* has been translated into English in many different ways ("one's own body," "body proper," "living body . . ."). Here, in order to remain consistent with Carbone's argumentations and closer to the French translation of *Leib* as "*corps propre*," each time a French philosopher will mention the Husserlian notion as "*corps propre*," I will use the expression "body proper," despite the various English translations appearing in the quoted writings—Trans.

22. J.-L. Nancy, *Corpus* (Paris: Métailié, 2000); trans. R. A. Rand, *Corpus* (New York: Fordham, 2008), 75.

23. M. Merleau-Ponty, *The Visible and the Invisible*, 147.

24. See J. Derrida, *Le toucher, Jean-Luc Nancy* (Paris: Galilée, 2000); trans. C. Irizarry, *On Touching—Jean-Luc Nancy* (Stanford: Stanford University Press, 2005), 184 and 356n33.

25. Ibid., 356n33.

26. See ibid.

27. R. Esposito, "Jean-Luc Nancy, il nucleo politico della filosofia," in *Il Manifesto* (June 10, 2000), 12. The text of this article is that of the Introduction to the international conference titled "Libertà in comune," organized by the Istituto Suor Orsola Benincasa in Naples, on June 9 and 10, 2000.

28. J.-L. Nancy, *Corpus*, 5. On the same issue, see also ibid., 27–28 and Nancy, *L'intrus* (Paris: Galilée, 2000); trans. R. A. Rand, "The Intruder," in Nancy, *Corpus*, 161–170.

29. See D. Franck, *Flesh and Body: On the Phenomenology of Husserl*, 84.

30. See ibid.: "My flesh extends as far as my perception extends: all the way to the stars." See also M. Merleau-Ponty, *The Visible and the Invisible*, 57, note 10. In consonance with Nancy's remarks on the "very familiar strangeness" of our body (see J.-L. Nancy, *Corpus*, 13), it is worth mentioning Merleau-Ponty's passage in whose conclusion he quotes Bergson: "What I 'am' I am only at a distance, yonder, in this body, this personage, these thoughts, which I push before myself and which are only my least remote distances (*mes lointains les moins éloignés*); and conversely I adhere to this world which is not me as closely as to myself, in a sense it is only the prolongation of my body" (M. Merleau-Ponty, *The Visible and the Invisible*, 57).

31. J. Derrida, *On Touching—Jean-Luc Nancy*, 233.

32. Ibid., 235.

33. M. Merleau-Ponty, "The Philosopher and His Shadow," in *Signs*, 167. Merleau-Ponty's pupil Waldenfels states that the notion of "flesh of the world" (which Merleau-Ponty himself expresses through the German *Leib der Welt*) can be considered as a "radicalization of the presence 'in person' (*leibhaftig*) that Husserl attributes to things in perception" (B. Waldenfels, *Phänomenologie in Frankreich*, 200).

34. J. Derrida, *On Touching—Jean-Luc Nancy*, 236.

35. M. Merleau-Ponty, "Themes from the Lectures at the Collège de France, 1952–1960," in *In Praise of Philosophy and Other Essays*, 190.

36. M. Henry, *Incarnation. Une philosophie de la chair* (Paris: Seuil, 2000).

37. Ibid., 7.

38. Ibid., 8.

39. Ibid., 9.

40. Ibid., 8.

41. Ibid., 10.

42. Ibid., 9.

43. Ibid., 10.

44. See ibid., 27.

45. See Tertullianus, *De carne Christi*, IX, 2.

46. "Quid caro quam terra conversa in figuras suas?" ["What is the flesh if not earth turned into forms belonging to it?"] (Tertullianus, *De carne Christi*, IX, 2).

47. M. Henry, *Incarnation. Une philosophie de la chair*, 27.

48. Ibid., 10.

49. Ibid., 27.

50. Ibid.

51. Ibid., 30.

52. See ibid., 31.

53. M. Heidegger, ed. W.-F. Von Herman, *Die Grundbegriffe der Metaphysik Welt—Endlichkeit—Einsamkeit* (Frankfurt am Main: Klostermann, 1983); trans. W. McNeill and N. Walker, *The Fundamental Concepts of Metaphysics: World, Finitude, Solitude* (Bloomington: Indiana University Press, 1995), § 47, 196.

54. For his part, Henry presents a Heideggerian statement with an analogous meaning: "According to Heidegger's profound observation, the table does not 'touch' the wall against which it is put. On the contrary, the peculiarity of a body like ours is that it feels every object close to it" (M. Henry, *Incarnation. Une philosophie de la chair*, 8).

55. J.-L. Nancy, *Le sens du monde* (Paris: Galilée, 1993); trans. J. S. Librett, *The Sense of the World* (Minneapolis: University of Minnesota Press, 1998), 62.

56. Ibid.

57. Ibid., 62–63. In relation to this Nancy argumentation, also see his *Corpus*, with a special reference to the paragraph titled "Aphallus and Acephale," 12–17. Here, he states precisely that bodies have "no head or tail" (that is, he denies their *organic* nature), and he affirms: "Bodies in the end *are* also that—head and tail: *the very discreteness of the sites of sense, of the moments of an organism, of the elements of matter.* The body is a place that opens, displaces and spaces phallus and cephale: *making room for them* to create an event" (ibid., 17).

58. M. Merleau-Ponty, *Nature*, 95.

59. Nancy specifies that the stone is "in the world in a way of being *in*, which is at least that of covering an area: extension, spacing, distance, 'atomic' constitution" (J-L. Nancy, *The Sense of the World*, 62).

60. J. Derrida, *On Touching—Jean-Luc Nancy*, 236.

61. "A philosophy of the flesh is the condition without which psychoanalysis remains anthropology" (M. Merleau-Ponty, *The Visible and the Invisible*, 267).

62. "The whole architecture of the notions of the psycho-logy [. . .] is suddenly clarified when one [. . .] think[s] all these terms [. . .] as *differentiations* of one sole and *massive* adhesion to Being which is the flesh [. . .]: for there is no *hierarchy* of orders or layers or planets (always founded on the individual-essence distinction), there is dimensionality of every fact and facticity of every dimension" (ibid., 270).

63. Ibid.

64. The title of the working note dated December 1960 is indeed "Body and flesh—Eros—Philosophy of Freudianism," see ibid., 269. For the proposal of an ontological interpretation of psychoanalysis, it is also important to mention Merleau-Ponty's "Preface" to the writing of the psychoanalyst A. Hesnard, *L'œuvre de Freud et son importance pour le monde moderne* (Paris: Payot, 1960); trans. A. L. Fisher, "Phenomenology and Psychoanalysis: Preface to Hesnard's L'Oeuvre de Freud," in *Review of Existential Psychology and Psychiatry* 18 (1982), 33–63; reprinted in Hesnard, ed. K. Hoeller, *Merleau-Ponty & Psychology* (Atlantic High-

lands, NJ: Humanities Press, 1993). I already discussed this subject in chapter 4 of my *Proust et les idées sensibles* (Paris: Vrin, 2008; trans. N. Keane, *An Unprecedented Deformation. Marcel Proust and the Sensible Ideas* [Albany: SUNY, 2010], 49–58), to which the reader can refer.

65. S. Freud, "Das Interesse an der Psychoanalyse," in *Scientia* 4, nos. 31 and 32 (1913); trans. J. Strachey, "The Claims of Psychoanalysis to Scientific Interest," in Freud, *The Standard Edition of the Complete psychological Works* (London: Hogarth Press, 1953–74), vol. 13, 165–190.

66. M. Merleau-Ponty, *The Visible and the Invisible*, 269.

67. See ibid., 267.

68. Although in the quoted working note the term *subject* occurs, Merleau-Ponty's ontology of the flesh explicitly implies a radical questioning of what this term traditionally designates.

69. M. Merleau-Ponty, *The Visible and the Invisible*, 270.

70. Ibid., 273.

71. Ibid., 270.

72. S. Freud, "Die Verdrängung," in *Internationale Zeitschrift für ärtztliche Psychoanalyse* 3, no. 3 (1915); trans. J. Strachey, "Repression," in Freud, *The Standard Edition of the Complete Psychological Works*, vol. 14, 150.

73. E. Husserl, "Foundational Investigations of the Phenomenological Origin of the Spatiality of Nature," 227, translation modified, my emphasis.

74. J.-P. Sartre, "Merleau-Ponty vivant," in *Les temps modernes* 184–185; trans. B. Eisher, "Merleau-Ponty *vivant*," in ed. J. Stewart, *The Debate Between Sartre and Merleau-Ponty* (Evanston: Northwestern University Press, 1998), 613.

75. J.-F. Lyotard, "Plusieurs silences" [1972] in Lyotard, *Des dispositifs pulsionnels* (Paris: Union Générale d'Édition, coll. 10/18, 1973); trans. J. Maier, "Several Silences," in Lyotard, *Driftworks*, 91.

76. J.-P. Sartre, "Merleau-Ponty *vivant*," in *Les temps modernes* 184–185, 613.

77. J.-L. Nancy, "Il taglio del senso—Intervista a Jean-Luc Nancy," in Nancy, *L'intrus*, Italian trans. and ed. V. Piazza, *L'intruso* (Napoli: Cronopio, 2000), 41.

78. J.-L. Nancy, "The Intruder" in Nancy, *Corpus*, 169.

79. Ibid., 163, my emphasis.

80. On the ethical and political implications of Merleau-Ponty's philosophical approaches, see ed. D. H. Davis, *Merleau-Ponty's Later Works and Their Practical Implications: The Dehiscence of Responsibility* (New York: Amherst, Humanity Books, 2001) and R. Bonan, *La dimension commune*, vol. 1, *Le problème de l'inter-subjectivité dans la philosophie de Merleau-Ponty*, vol. 2, *L'institution intersubjective comme poétique générale* (Paris: l'Harmattan, 2001).

81. In virtue of one of those operations of "sharing" between the two philosophers highlighted by Derrida in *On Touching—Jean-Luc Nancy*. See, in particular, 218.

82. R. Esposito, "Jean-Luc Nancy, il nucleo politico della filosofia," in *Il Manifesto*, June 10, 2000, my emphasis.

83. M. Merleau-Ponty, *The Visible and the Invisible*, 264.

84. Concerning the historically *plural* characterization of the notion of "globalization" [*"globalisation"*] that I meant to suggest here, see Jacques Le Goff's communication at the *Forum* of the *Académie universelle des cultures*, which took place in Paris on November 13 and 14, 2001. In the version published on "Le Monde" we can read that: "The knowledge of the previous forms of globalization [*mondialisation*] is necessary in order to understand those we experience and to adopt the most convenient policy when facing this phenomenon" (J. Le Goff, "Heurs et malheurs des mondialisations," in *Le Monde*, November 16, 2001, 1 and 17).

85. See R. Esposito and J.-L. Nancy, *Dialogo sulla filosofia a venire* [Introduction to the Italian edition of J.-L. Nancy, *Être singulier pluriel* (Paris: Galilée, 1996); Italian trans. D. Tarizzo, *Essere singolare plurale* (Torino: Einaudi, 2001), VII–XXIX]; trans. T. Campbell, in *Minnesota Review* 75 (Fall 2010), 71–88.

86. Ibid., 87, trans. modified.

87. Ibid., 85–86.

88. P. Montani, *Bioestetica. Senso comune, tecnica e arte nell'età della globalizzazione* (Roma: Carocci, 2007), 15.

89. R. Diodato, *Estetica del virtuale* (Milano: Mondadori, 2005); trans. J. L. Harmon, rev. and ed. S. Benso, *Aesthetics of the Virtual* (New York: SUNY, 2012), X, translation modified.

90. Ibid., 65.

91. Ibid.

Chapter Two

1. M. Merleau-Ponty, *La prose du monde*, text established and presented by C. Lefort (Paris: Tel-Gallimard, 1969); trans. J. O'Neill, *The Prose of the World* (Evanston: Northwestern University Press, 1973). In his "Editor's Preface," Claude Lefort provides some precious information on the history of this book and casts a light on a particularly important moment in Merleau-Ponty's intellectual itinerary. Concerning the dates of the writing of *The Prose of the World*, Lefort inclines us to think that the pages that were found—which should constitute the first part of the work—have been written, on the basis of previous spurs, during a single year, namely 1951. The decision to suspend the writing was probably made at the beginning of the following year. It is also to be remarked that, between 1950 and 1951, Merleau-Ponty decided to reduce, in relation to his previous projects, the thematic field of *The Prose of the World*. As Lefort suggests, this probably happened because Merleau-Ponty meant to subordinate such a thematic field to that of *The Origin of Truth*, namely, the book to which he meant to assign the task of revealing the ontological sense of his theory of expression. The reflections concerning the themes this work should have focused on eventually converged in the unfinished pages of *The Visible and the Invisible*. Concerning the same phase of Merleau-Ponty's thought, see below, n63 to Chapter Four, 103.

2. M. Merleau-Ponty, *The Prose of the World*, 147.

3. Ibid., 152.

4. M. Merleau-Ponty, *The Visible and the Invisible*, 218. Merleau-Ponty uses the expression "skin of things," explicitly referring to Paul Klee's painting in his *Notes de cours au Collège de France 1958–1959 et 1960–1961*, 56. I will get back to these references in the next chapter of the present work.

5. See J. Derrida, *On touching—Jean-Luc Nancy*, in particular, 198.

6. Ibid., 188.

7. Ibid., 233.

8. K. Varnedoe, "Gauguin," in ed. W. Rubin, *"Primitivism" in 20th Century Art: Affinity of the Tribal and the Modern* (New York: The Museum of Modern Art, 1984), vol. I, 179.

9. M. Merleau-Ponty, *Signs*, 181. Here Merleau-Ponty significantly points out the convergence of the phenomenological enterprise—in which he feels engaged himself—and the enterprise developed, in his opinion, by modern painting. As he writes: "Willy-nilly, against his plans and according to his essential audacity, Husserl awakens a wild-flowering world and mind. Things are no longer there simply according to their projective appearances and the requirements of the panorama, as in Renaissance perspective; but on the contrary upright, insistent, flaying our glance with their edges, each thing claiming an absolute presence which is not compossible with the absolute presence of the other things, and which they nevertheless have all together by virtue of a configurational meaning which is no way indicated by its 'theoretical meaning.'" I will get back to this passage in the next chapter.

10. M. Merleau-Ponty, *Notes de cours au Collège de France 1958–1959 et 1960–1961*, 155.

11. *"The brute or wild Being (= the perceived world)"* (M. Merleau-Ponty, *The Visible and the Invisible*, 170, my emphasis).

12. Ibid., my emphasis.

13. P. Gauguin, "Huysmans et Redon" [1889], in Gauguin, *Oviri. Écrits d'un sauvage*; trans. E. Levieux, "Huysmans and Redon," in Gauguin, ed. D. Guérin, *The Writings of a Savage* (New York: Da Capo Press, 1996), 39.

14. P. Gauguin, "Miscellaneous Things" [1896–1897], in *The Writings of a Savage*, 145.

15. P. Gauguin, "Notes on Art at the Universal Exhibition" [1889], in *The Writings of a Savage*, 30.

16. Ibid., 31, translation modified, my emphasis.

17. P. Gauguin, "Notes synthétiques" [1884–1885], in *The Writings of a Savage*, 11, translation modified.

18. P. Gauguin, "Notebook for Aline" [1892], in *The Writings of a Savage*, 67.

19. The expression *"reprise créatrice"* is Merleau-Pontian. See, for instance, M. Merleau-Ponty, *Sens et non sens* [1948] (Paris: Gallimard, 1996); trans. H. and P. Dreyfus (Evanston: Northwestern University Press, 1964), 25. See also "Un

inédit de Merleau-Ponty" [1952] in Merleau-Ponty, *Parcours deux (1951–61)* (Lagrasse: Verdier, 2000), 43.

20. M. Merleau-Ponty, *The Visible and the Invisible*, 267, and *Nature*, 38.

21. M. Merleau-Ponty, *Nature*, 38.

22. P. Gauguin, "Miscellaneous Things," in *The Writings of a Savage*, 144.

23. "It is good for the young to have a model, but let them draw a curtain over it while they paint it" (P. Gauguin, "Notebook for Aline," in *The Writings of a Savage*, 91).

24. Ibid.

25. K. Varnedoe, "Gauguin," in *"Primitivism" in 20th Century Art: Affinity of the Tribal and the Modern*, 185.

26. Ibid. The reference is to the following passage from "Miscellaneous Things": "Japanese sketches, Hokusai prints, Daumier lithographs, [cruel observations by] Forain, the school of Giotto, brought together [in an album], not by chance but by my [good] will, altogether intentionally. [. . .] Because they appear to be different, I want to show how they are related" (P. Gauguin, "Miscellaneous Things," in *The Writings of a Savage*, 131).

27. See K. Varnedoe, "Gauguin," in *"Primitivism" in 20th Century Art: Affinity of the Tribal and the Modern*, 185 ff.

28. Ibid., 191.

29. Ibid.

30. P. Gauguin, ed. P. Verdier, "L'esprit moderne et le catholicisme," in *Wallral-Richartz Jahrbuch*, XLVI, 1985, 273–278. I would like to thank Elizabeth C. Childs for sending me this edition of the manuscript.

31. J. Derrida, *On touching—Jean-Luc Nancy*, 219. For his part, Jean-Luc Nancy explains that in his opinion Christianity deconstructs itself "insofar as it comes undone from religion, from its legend and its belief" (J.-L. Nancy, *Visitation (de la peinture chrétienne)* [Paris: Galilée, 2001]; trans. J. Fort, "Visitation: of Christian Painting," in Nancy, *The Ground of the Image* [New York: Fordham University Press, 2005], 123). See also ibid., 124.

32. P. Gauguin, *Noa Noa* (Paris: G. Crès et C., 1929); trans. O. F. Theis, *Noa Noa* (New York: The Noonday Press, 1957), 10.

33. P. Gauguin, *Noa Noa*, 33.

34. P. Gauguin, "Noa Noa," in *The Writings of a Savage*, 99.

35. P. Gauguin, ed. M. Malingue, *Lettres de Gauguin à sa femme et à ses amis* (Paris: Grasset, 1946); trans. H. J. Stenning, *Paul Gauguin: Letters to His Wife and Friends* (London: The Saturn Press, 1949), 216.

36. P. Gauguin, "Miscellaneous Things," in *The Writings of a Savage*, 133, my emphasis.

37. A. G. Barskaja, M. A. Bessanova, *Capolavori impressionisti e postimpressionisti dai musei sovietici* (Milano: Electa, 1983), 66. On the same subject, see also B. Dorival, "Sources of the Art of Gauguin from Java, Egypt and Ancient Greece," in *Burlington Magazine* 577 (April 1951), 118–122, in particular, 121–122.

38. K. Varnedoe, "Gauguin," in *"Primitivism" in 20th Century Art: Affinity of the Tribal and the Modern*, 190.

39. See the extracts from P. Gauguin, "The Catholic Church and Modern Times," [1897] in *The Writings of a Savage*, 163–166.

40. Ibid., 163.

41. J.-L. Nancy, *Le regard du portrait* (Paris: Galilée, 2000); trans. S. Sparks, "The Look of the Portrait," in Nancy, *Multiple Arts: The Muses* II (Stanford: Stanford University Press, 2006), 240–241.

42. J.-L. Nancy, "Visitation/Of Christian Painting," in *The Ground of the Image*, 123.

43. M. Merleau-Ponty, *Le Visible et l'invisible*, 148.

44. Ibid.

45. "It is necessary to question on this '*incarnat*,' starting with the impossible understanding of the word. *In*, is this inside, is this on? And the *carne*, the *chair* [= flesh], isn't this what in any case designates the absolute bloody, the shapeless, the inside of the body, opposed to its white surface? Then why do the *chairs* [= fleshes] find themselves constantly invoked, in the painters' texts, to designate their Other, namely, the *skin*?" (G. Didi-Huberman, *La Peinture incarnée* [Paris: Minuit, 1985], 22). Nancy adds: "painting is the art of bodies, in that it only knows about skin, being skin through and through" (J.-L. Nancy, *Corpus*, 15).

46. J.-L. Nancy, *The Look of the Portrait*, 240.

47. J. L. Nancy, "Visitation: Of Christian Painting," in *The Ground of the Image*, 123.

48. E. Panofsky, *Idea: Ein Beitrag zur Begriffsgeschichte der älteren Kunsttheorie* (Leipzig: Teubner, 1924); trans., J. Peake, *Idea: A Concept in Art Theory* (Columbia: University South Carolina Press, 1968), 31, my emphasis.

49. M. Merleau-Ponty, *Signs*, 167.

50. Kirk Varnedoe writes that in *Manao Tupapau* Tehamana actually is "a variant of Manet's *Olympia*, inverted and exoticized to be more alluringly acquiescent" (K. Varnedoe, "Gauguin," in *"Primitivism" in 20th Century Art: Affinity of the Tribal and the Modern*, 199).

51. Such a sensibility strongly emerges in P. Gauguin, "The Catholic Church and Modern Times," in *The Writings of a Savage*, in particular, 163–164.

52. See M. Merleau-Ponty, *Notes de cours au Collège de France 1958–1959 et 1960–1961*, 277. See F. Nietzsche, "Die frohliche Wissenschaft" [1887], in ed. G. Colli, M. Montinari, *Nietzsche Werke: Kritische Gesamtausgabe*, part 5, vol. 2 (Berlin: Walter de Gruyter, 1973); trans. W. Kaufmann, *The Gay Science* (New York: Vintage Books, 1974), 38.

53. On this issue, see K. Varnedoe, "Gauguin," in *"Primitivism" in 20th Century Art: Affinity of the Tribal and the Modern*, 183–184 and 199–200.

54. See ibid., 199.

55. This is indeed confirmed by Merleau-Ponty where he focuses on the characteristics of the Eskimo masks through some remarks precisely recalling the notion of "flesh of the world." See M. Merleau-Ponty, *Nature*, 306n16, and 307n11.

56. K. Varnedoe, "Gauguin," in *"Primitivism" in 20th Century Art: Affinity of the Tribal and the Modern*, 201.

57. M. Merleau-Ponty, "Themes from the Lectures at the Collège de France, 1952–1960," in Merleau-Ponty, *In Praise of Philosophy and Other Essays*, 116.

Chapter Three

1. P. Klee, "Schöpferische Konfession," in ed. K. Edschmid, *Tribune der Kunst und Zeit*, 13 (Berlin: Erich Reiss, 1920); trans. N. Guterman, "Creative Credo," in ed. H. B. Chipp, *Theories of Modern Art: A Source Book by Artists and Critics* (Berkeley: University of California Press, 1973), 182–186, here 182.

2. Ibid., 185. See also M. Merleau-Ponty, *Notes des cours au Collège de France 1958–1959 et 1960–1961*, 56na.

3. P. Klee, *Über die moderne Kunst* [1924] (Bern-Bümpliz: Benteli, 1945); trans. P. Findlay, with an introduction by H. Read, *On Modern Art* (London: Faber and Faber, 1987), 45. See also M. Merleau-Ponty, *Notes des cours au Collège de France 1958–1959 et 1960–1961*, 58. On the philosophical issues raised by such a declaration, see E. Franzini, *I simboli e l'invisibile. Figure e forme del pensiero simbolico* (Milano: il Saggiatore, 2008). Franzini quotes Klee's sentence and comments on it (101 and ff.).

4. M. Merleau-Ponty, *Phénoménologie de la perception* [1945] (Paris: Gallimard, 1992); trans. D. A. Landes, *Phenomenology of Perception* (London: Routledge Chapman & Hall, 2012), XXXV. As for me, I think that the dynamics of change to which Merleau-Ponty refers in the complex of his work concern an epoch which is still our own. This is why I will qualify it as "contemporary." I will characterize it just in the same way as the cultural symptoms, which, in my opinion, highlight those dynamics, although they are defined as "modern" by the tradition of their own discipline or by the authors who have studied them. Instead, I shall call "modern" the cultural paradigm that such dynamics tend to question.

5. Apropos of such a convergence, some issues concerning the theme of the visible are recalled by C. Fontana in his essay "Fenomenografie. Paul Klee e il segreto pittografico della creazione," in ed. C. Fontana, *Paul Klee. Preistoria del visibile* (Milano: Silvana Editoriale, 1996), 97–98. Other issues, concerning color, are the subject of the article by G. A. Johnson, "Thinking in Color: Merleau-Ponty and Paul Klee," in ed. V. M. Fòti, *Merleau-Ponty: Difference, Materiality, Painting* (Atlantic Highlands, NJ: Humanities Press, 1996), 169–176. More issues, concerning the time of the work of art, are discussed in another article by G. A. Johnson, "The Presence of the Artwork. A Past that Is not Past: Merleau-Ponty and Paul Klee," in eds. D. Morris and K. Maclaren, *Time, Memory, and Institution: Merleau-Ponty's New Ontology of the Self* (Athens, OH: Ohio University Press, 2015), 238–253. Moreover, some issues concerning beauty are the subject of the chapter titled "Paul Klee: Mortal Beauty," in Johnson's book *The Retrieval of the*

Beautiful: Thinking Through Merleau-Ponty's Aesthetics (Evanston: Northwestern University Press, 2010), 103–141.

6. See M. Merleau-Ponty, *Notes de cours au Collège de France 1958–1959 et 1960–1961*, 52–61. See also W. Grohmann, *Paul Klee* [1954], trans. N. Guterman (New York: Harry N. Abrams, 1955).

7. See M. Merleau-Ponty, *Notes de cours au Collège de France 1958–1959 et 1960–1961*, 61.

8. Ibid., 58.

9. M. Merleau-Ponty, "Themes from the Lectures at the Collège de France, 1952–1960," 197.

10. Ibid., 167.

11. See M. Merleau-Ponty, *Eye and Mind*, 132 (the English translation renders *voyance* as *visualization*).

12. M. Merleau-Ponty, *Notes de cours au Collège de France 1958–1959 et 1960–1961*, 391.

13. "Paul Klee's four-volume pedagogical journals were edited and published in German in 1956, and appeared in French translation in 1959, where Merleau-Ponty read them. In writing *Eye and Mind* in 1960, Merleau-Ponty studied Klee's *Journals*, and that artist emerges as one of the strongest new voices in Merleau-Ponty's last theory of painting and *Naturphilosophie*" (G. A. Johnson, "Thinking in Color: Merleau-Ponty and Paul Klee," 170).

14. M. Merleau-Ponty, *Notes de cours au Collège de France 1958–1959 et 1960–1961*, 191.

15. See ibid., 391. "All in all—Merleau-Ponty remarks further on—Proust: carnal essences; Valéry: conscience is not in immanence, but in life; Claudel: simultaneity, the most real is *beneath* us; St J Perse: Poetry as an awakening to the Being; Cl Simon: the zone of credulity and the zone of the sensible being. [There is] reversal of the relations between the visible and the invisible; of flesh and mind; discovery of a signification as nervure of the full Being; surpassing of the minds' insularity" (ibid., 392).

16. G. Charbonnier, *Le Monologue du peintre, I* (Paris: Julliard, 1959), 34. Max Ernst's declaration is already echoed in *The Visible and the Invisible*, 208, and quoted in *Eye and Mind*, 128–129. On this subject, the reader can refer to my *La Visibilité de l'invisible. Merleau-Ponty entre Cézanne et Proust* (Hildesheim: Georg Olms Verlag, 2001), 110–118.

17. M. Merleau-Ponty, *Notes de cours au Collège de France 1958–1959 et 1960–1961*, 190.

18. Ibid., 175.

19. Ibid., 390.

20. M. Merleau-Ponty, *Signs*, 20.

21. Merleau-Ponty, *Notes de cours au Collège de France 1958–1959 et 1960–1961*, 183, translation modified.

22. Ibid., 175.

23. M. Merleau-Ponty, *Eye and Mind*, 253. Merleau-Ponty analyses the literary expression of simultaneity, starting in particular from the sentence concluding the *Recherche* (see *Notes de cours au Collège de France 1958–1959 et 1960–1961*, 197), from Claudel's pages (see ibid., 198 and ff.) and from Claude Simon (see ibid., 204 and ff.), as it is pointed out in the quotation reported in note 15 of the present chapter.

24. M. Merleau-Ponty, *Notes de cours au Collège de France 1958–1959 et 1960–1961*, 183.

25. Ibid., 182–183, my emphasis.

26. Ibid., 183.

27. M. Merleau-Ponty, *Eye and Mind*, 132.

28. Ibid., 124. Christine Buci-Glucksmann points out that Merleau-Ponty contributes to the elaboration, by his conception of *voyance*, of a notion exceeding "sight, [. . .] an aspect of the visual that is liberated from the context of the optic-representative" (C. Buci-Glucksmann, *La folie du voir. De l'esthétique baroque* [Paris: Galilée, 1986]; trans. D. Z. Baker, *The Madness of Vision. On Baroque aesthetics* [Athens, OH: Ohio University Press], 24).

29. Significantly, in *Eye and Mind* the sensible universe is defined as "the oneiric world of analogy" (M. Merleau-Ponty, *Eye and Mind*, 132).

30. E. Husserl, "Formale und transzendentale Logik. Versuch einer Kritik der logischen Vernunft," in *Jahrbuch für Philosophie und phänomenologische Forschung*, X (1929); trans. D. Cairns, *Formal and Transcendental Logic* (The Hague: Martinus Nijhoff, 1969), 292. We might remember that Rimbaud also theorizes the poet's becoming *voyant* "by a long, gigantic, and rational *derangement of all the senses*" (A. Rimbaud, *Rimbaud. Complete Works, Selected Letters*; trans. with an introduction and notes by W. Fowlie, updated and with a foreword by S. Whidden [Chicago-London: University of Chicago Press 1966–2005], 307). "This does not mean not to think anymore—the derangement of the senses is the breaking down of the divisions between them in order to rediscover their indivision—And that way, a thought that is not *mine, but theirs*" (M. Merleau-Ponty, *Notes de cours au Collège de France 1958–1959 et 1960–1961*, 186, my emphasis). For the confrontation that this may open up, we shall also recall how Gilles Deleuze saw in this formulation of Rimbaud's a possible summary of the *Critique of Judgment*: the "formula of a profoundly romantic Kant" (G. Deleuze, *Critique et clinique* [Paris: Minuit, 1993]; trans. D. W. Smith and M. A. Greco, *Essays Critical and Clinical* [London–New York: Verso, 1998], 33).

31. See P. Klee, "Survey and Orientation in Regard to Pictorial Elements and Their Spatial Arrangement," in *The Notebooks of Paul Klee*, Vol. I: *The Thinking Eye*, 90 ("This acceptance [. . .] of the object"). In German *Jawort* is a "yes" as a matrimonial assent. See also M. Merleau-Ponty, *Notes de cours au Collège de France 1958–1959 et 1960–1961*, 59na.

32. P. Claudel, *L'œil écoute* (1946) (Paris: Gallimard, 1990); trans. E. Pell, *The Eye Listens* (New York: Philosophical Library 1950). In the part of his working notes on Claudel, whom he includes among the writers "reintroducing, more vio-

lently, [Proust's] very enterprise," Merleau-Ponty refers precisely to *The Eye Listens*, remarking as follows: "anti-Platonism: of course, the visible is not all—still, what is truer than it is, that is its double or shadow" (M. Merleau-Ponty, *Notes de cours au Collège de France 1958–1959 et 1960–1961*, respectively, 198 and 201 and ff).

33. On this issue, see also M. Dufrenne, *L'œil et l'oreille* (Montreal: Éditions de l'Hexagone, 1987), 115.

34. M. Merleau-Ponty, *Eye and Mind*, 139, translation modified.

35. M. Merleau-Ponty, *The Visible and the Invisible*, 218. The parallel between contemporary music and painting is developed by Merleau-Ponty in his *Notes de cours au Collège de France 1958–1959 et 1960–1961*, 61–64.

36. M. Merleau-Ponty, *Notes de cours au Collège de France 1958–1959 et 1960–1961*, 56.

37. See the letter to Mersenne of November 20, 1629 in R. Descartes, ed. A. Tannery, *Œuvres* (Paris: Vrin, 1996); trans. A. Kenny in ed. A. Kenny, *Descartes: Philosophical Letters* (Oxford: Clarendon Press, 1970), 3–6.

38. M. Merleau-Ponty, *Notes de cours au Collège de France 1958–1959 et 1960–1961*, 183. This equivalence is already affirmed in *Eye and Mind*, 389n22 "the systems of means by which painting makes us see is a scientific matter. Why, then, do we not methodically produce perfect images of the world, arriving at a universal art purged of personal art, just as the universal language would free us of all the confused relationships that lurk in existent languages?"

39. M. Merleau-Ponty, *Notes de cours au Collège de France 1958–1959 et 1960–1961*, 186.

40. Ibid., 187.

41. Ibid.

42. See ibid., 189.

43. See ibid., 186 and, for the Rimbaud quotation, see his letter *To Georges Izambard* of May 13, 1871, considered as a draft of the *Lettre du voyant*, in A. Rimbaud, *Complete Works, Selected Letters*, 303–304. In the 1951 lecture titled "Man and Adversity," later published in *Signs*, Merleau-Ponty already anticipates this opinion on the poetic experiences inaugurated by the *Lettre du voyant*, declaring among other things that "[l]iterature has long taken exception to ordinary language. As different as the ventures of Rimbaud and Mallarmé may well have been, they had this much in common: they freed language from the control of 'obvious facts' and trusted it to invent and win new relationships of meaning. Thus language ceased to be (if it ever has been) simply a tool or means the writer uses to communicate intentions given independently of language. In our day, language is of a piece with the writer; it is the writer himself. It is no longer the servant of significations, but the act of signifying itself, and the writer or man speaking no longer has to control it voluntarily any more than living man has to premeditate the means or details of his gestures; [. . .] As a professional of language, the writer is a professional of insecurity" (M. Merleau-Ponty, *Signs*), 232. To open up more comparison perspectives, we could flag Heidegger's interest in Rimbaud, which some texts emerging from the exchange with Réné Char witness. Among such

texts, see in particular M. Heidegger, "Rimbaud vivant," in *Aus der Erfahrung des Denkens, Gesamtausgabe*, vol. 13 (Frankfurt am Main: Klostermann, 1983), 225–227, translation modified.

44. C. Buci-Glucksmann, *The Madness of Vision: On Baroque Aesthetics*, 25.

45. M. Richir, "Essences et 'intuition' des essences chez le dernier Merleau-Ponty," in *Phénomènes, temps et êtres. Ontologie et phénoménologie* (Grenoble: Million, 1987), 79.

46. On this subject, we are reminded of the critique of Husserl's "myth" of a disincarnated *Wesensschau* operated by a "pure spectator"—a critique that Merleau-Ponty develops in the chapter "Interrogation and Intuition" of *The Visible and the Invisible* (see, in particular, 116). Moreover, in a working note of the same text, he writes: "seeing is this sort of thought that has no need to think in order to possess the *Wesen*" (ibid., 247).

47. M. Merleau-Ponty, *The Visible and the Invisible*, 266.

48. Ibid., 101, my emphasis.

49. In the notes for the course on Paul Klee, whilst remarking that the "irony" of the painter "may even be a philosophy" (needless to say, an implicit one), Merleau-Ponty questions: "Is there *possession* of being through philosophy?" (M. Merleau-Ponty, *Notes de cours au Collège de France 1958–1959 et 1960–1961*, 58).

50. M. Merleau-Ponty, *The Visible and the Invisible*, 102.

51. M. Merleau-Ponty, *Signs*, 78.

52. In this sense—as Merleau-Ponty writes in a working note significantly titled "Philosophy and Literature"—such a work of creation "is hence a creation in a radical sense: a creation that is at the same time an adequation, the only way to obtain an adequation" (M. Merleau-Ponty, *The Visible and the Invisible*, 197). Concerning the affinities between this conception of creation and Klee's idea of "making visible," the following text may be consulted: C. Fontana, "Fenomeno-grafie. Paul Klee e il segreto pittografico della creazione," 99 and ff.

53. M. Merleau-Ponty, "Themes from the Lectures at the Collège de France, 1952–1960," 118.

54. M. Merleau-Ponty, *The Visible and the Invisible*, 266. See also another often quoted passage from the same text: "[h]e who cannot possess the visible unless he is possessed by it, unless he is *of it*" (ibid., 134–135). It seems to me that this sentence confirms that the problem, for Merleau-Ponty, is not so much getting to a revocation of all will for possession, but rather getting to the recognition of an original and irreducible reciprocity of such possession.

55. See the passage quoted above, n9 to Chapter Two, 93. Moreover, we shall keep in mind Merleau-Ponty's already recalled comparison between the Renaissance theory of perspective and the Cartesian idea of a universal language (see above, n43 to Chapter Three, 99).

56. Deleuze highlights the "affinity" between Klee and the Baroque (G. Deleuze, *Le pli. Leibniz et le Baroque* [Paris: Minuit, 1988]; trans. T. Conley, *The Fold: Leibniz and the Baroque* [Minneapolis: University of Minnesota Press, 1993]). On the baroque inspiration linking Deleuze and Merleau-Ponty, see P. Gam-

bazzi, "La piega e il pensiero. Sull'ontologia di Merleau-Ponty," *aut aut* 262–263 (1994) 21–47. In her turn, Christine Buci-Glucksmann thematized the closeness between the aesthetic ontology of the later Merleau-Ponty and the ontological aesthetics of the Baroque. See C. Buci-Glucksmann, *The Madness of Vision*, 26 and 33–34.

57. M. Merleau-Ponty, *Signs*, 181.

58. "Partout et nulle part" is composed of six sections which constitute the preface and the introductions to five chapters of the collective work *Les philosophes célèbres*, edited by Merleau-Ponty (Paris: Mazenod, 1956). It was later published in *Signs*.

59. M. Merleau-Ponty, *Signs*, 138.

60. Ibid.

61. Ibid.

62. M. Merleau-Ponty, *The Visible and the Invisible*, 221.

63. M. Perniola, "Presentazione," in B. Gracián, *Agudeza y arte de ingenio* (1648), Italian trans. G. Poggi (Palermo: Aesthetica, 1986), 19. See also the connection between Merleau-Ponty and Gracián proposed by C. Buci-Glucksmann, *The Madness of Vision*, 28.

64. J. Taminiaux, "Les tensions internes de la *Critique du Jugement*," in *La nostalgie de la Grèce à l'aube de l'idéalisme allemand. Kant et les Grecs dans l'itinéraire de Schiller, de Hölderlin et de Hegel* (The Hague: M. Nijhoff, 1977), 61. On the same subject, the reader can refer once more to my *La visibilité de l'invisible. Merleau-Ponty entre Cézanne et Proust*, 151–170.

Chapter Four

1. M. Merleau-Ponty, *Sens et Non-Sens* (Paris: Nagel, 1948); trans. H. Dreyfus and P. Dreyfus, *Sense and Non-Sense* (Evanston: Northwestern University Press, 1964).

2. M. Merleau-Ponty, "Le cinéma et la nouvelle psychologie" (1947); trans. H. Dreyfus and P. Dreyfus, "The Film and the New Psychology," in *Sense and Non-Sense*, 48–59.

3. Ibid., 49.

4. Ibid., 50.

5. Ibid.

6. Ibid, 50–51.

7. Ibid., 52.

8. Ibid.

9. Ibid.

10. Ibid., 54.

11. Ibid.

12. E. Paci, "Introduzione" to M. Merleau-Ponty, *Senso e non senso*; Italian trans. P. Caruso (Milano: Il Saggiatore, 1962; later Milano: Garzanti 1974), 13.

13. M. Merleau-Ponty, *Sense and Non-Sense*, 54.

14. Ibid.

15. Ibid.

16. See P. Rodrigo, "Merleau-Ponty. Du cinéma à la peinture: le 'vouloir-dire' et l'expression élémentaire" (2005), in Rodrigo, *L'intentionnalité créatrice. Problèmes de phénoménologie et d'esthétique*, 235–255.

17. Ibid., 250.

18. Ibid.

19. Ibid., 252.

20. Ibid., 253.

21. Ibid.

22. See ibid., 23. Merleau-Ponty, *Sense and Non-Sense*, 54.

24. This is what Jean-Pierre Charcosset remarks in his *Merleau-Ponty. Approches phénoménologiques* (Paris: Hachette, 1981), 23.

25. Merleau-Ponty, *Sense and Non-Sense*, 48.

26. On this subject, see J.-P. Sartre, "Défense et illustration d'un Art international" (1924 or 1925), in Sartre, eds. M. Contat, M. Rybalka, *Écrits de jeunesse* (Paris: Gallimard, 1990), 390: "One can [. . .] apply [to cinema] what Bergson elsewhere said about music."

27. Merleau-Ponty, *Sense and Non-Sense*, 49.

28. Ibid., 54, my emphasis.

29. Ibid.

30. See M. Merleau-Ponty, *Phénoménologie de la perception* (Paris, 1945); trans. C. Smith, *Phenomenology of Perception* (London: Routledge, 1962; revised, 1981), 182–183.

31. M. Proust, eds. P. Clarac and A. Ferré, *À la Recherche du temps perdu*, vol. I: "Du côté de chez Swann" (Paris: Bibliothèque de la Plèiade, 1954); trans. C. K. Scott-Moncrieff, *Remembrance of Things Past*, vol. I: "Swann's Way" (London: Wordsworth Editions, 2006), 334.

32. M. Merleau-Ponty, *Sense and Non-Sense*, 49.

33. Ibid., translation modified.

34. H. Bergson, *L'évolution créatrice* (Paris: Alcan, 1907); trans. A. Mitchell, *Creative Evolution* (London: Macmillan, 1954), 322–323.

35. M. Merleau-Ponty, *Sense and Non-Sense*, 54.

36. Ibid., 55.

37. Maurice Jaubert, the most important cinema musician in France before the Second World War, quoted by Merleau-Ponty in ibid., 56.

38. J.-P. Charcosset, *Merleau-Ponty. Approches phénoménologiques*, 22.

39. M. Merleau-Ponty, *Sense and Non-Sense*, 57.

40. I. Kant, *Kritik der Urteilskraft* (Berlin u. Libau: Lagarde u. Friedrich,1790); trans. P. Guyer, E. Matthews, ed. P. Guyer, *Critique of the Power of Judgment* (Cambridge: Cambridge University Press, 2000), 192.

41. M. Merleau-Ponty, *Sense and Non-Sense*, 57.

42. Ibid., 57–58.

43. Ibid., 53–54.

44. M. Proust, *Remembrance of Things Past*, vol. I: "Swann's Way," 334, my emphasis.

45. M. Merleau-Ponty, *Sense and Non-Sense*, 58.

46. Ibid.

47. Ibid., 49.

48. Ibid., p. 59.

49. C. Metz, *Essais sur la signification au cinema* (Paris, 1968); trans. M. Taylor, *Film Language. A Semiotics of the Cinema*, (New York: Oxford University Press, 1974), 42–43. I owe the recommendation of this passage to Anna Caterina Dalmasso, whom I take here the opportunity to thank.

50. Ibid.

51. Merleau-Ponty, *Sense and Non-Sense*, 58.

52. See S. Kristensen, "Maurice Merleau-Ponty, une esthétique du mouvement," in *Archives de Philosophie* 69 (2006), 137n31.

53. M. Merleau-Ponty, J.-L. Godard (propos recueillis par), "Le testament de Balthazar," *Cahiers du cinéma* 177 (1966), 58–59.

54. M. Merleau-Ponty, *Notes de cours au Collège de France 1958–1959 et 1960–1961*, 390–391.

55. Ibid., 391. Here, the expression "fundamental thinking" indicates precisely a kind of "spontaneous philosophy," of "thinking of the *Ungedachte*" (ibid.), where a relation between humanity and Being is at work, which philosophical thinking has not yet properly *thought*.

56. Ibid.

57. Ibid.

58. Ibid. For putting into perspective the combination of the birth of cinema and the heritage of the philosophical reflection on movement, see P. Montebello, *Deleuze, philosophie et cinéma* (Paris: Vrin, 2008), 11–16.

59. M. Merleau-Ponty, *Notes de cours au Collège de France 1958–1959 et 1960–1961*, 166.

60. M. Merleau-Ponty, *The Visible and the Invisible*, 157.

61. M. Merleau-Ponty, *Eye and Mind*, 144–145.

62. M. Merleau-Ponty, *In Praise of Philosophy and Other Essays,* 78.

63. Saint Aubert refers to such a transcription in his essay titled "Conscience et expression chez Merleau-Ponty," in *Chiasmi* 10 (2008), 85–106. He points out that "[t]his document has a privileged position in the evolution of Merleau-Ponty's philosophical work. First of all, along with the *Recherches sur l'usage littéraire du langage* [*Studies in the Literary Use of Language*], it is the first course at the Collège de France: Merleau-Ponty put a remarkable attention in its preparation, whose length corresponds to about 130 pages of an ordinary edition. The date is also very important: we are in early 1953, that is, just after the thesis period, which ended in 1945, after the author's most existentialist phase (1945–1949), and following three years of courses at the Sorbonne (1950–1952). These last two periods witnessed the birth of the notion of flesh and the emergence of the theme of expression, particularly in the unpublished

preparation of the lectures given in Mexico City in early 1949, and, two years later, in the lecture on *L'homme et l'adversité* [*Man and Adversity*] and in the writing of the fundamental manuscript *La prose du monde* [*The Prose of the World*]. By its very title, the course on The Sensible World and the World of Expression realizes the junction between the major theme of Merleau-Ponty's main thesis—i.e., perception—and that, which is hence more recent, of expression" (ibid., 85–86). See also E. de Saint Aubert, "Conscience et expression. Avant-propos," in M. Merleau-Ponty, eds. E. de Saint Aubert, S. Kristensen, *Le monde sensible et le monde de l'expression. Cours au Collège de France. Notes, 1953* (Geneva: MêtisPresses, 2011), 7–38.

64. Kristensen refers to this transcription in his essay titled "Maurice Merleau-Ponty, une esthétique du mouvement," 123–146. Here he significantly announces that, by examining Merleau-Ponty's course notes, his essay aims at focusing "on the Merleau-Pontian phenomenology of movement, [and on its] relations to cinema" so as to get to "Jean-Luc Godard's relation to phenomenology and to indicate the premises of a dialogue concerning Deleuze's approach to cinema" (ibid., 123).

65. M. Merleau-Ponty, *In Praise of Philosophy and Other Essays*, 73, trans. modified.

66. Ibid.

67. See M. Merleau-Ponty, *Le monde sensible et le monde de l'expression. Cours au Collège de France. Notes, 1953*, 66, 68, 93, 97.

68. M. Merleau-Ponty, *Phenomenology of Perception*, 283. See also ibid., 287, where Merleau-Ponty writes, with reference to Wertheimer: "[t]he psychologist leads us back to this phenomenal layer. We shall not say that it is irrational or anti-logical. This would only be the positioning of a movement without a mobile" (translation modified).

69. See M. Merleau-Ponty, *Le monde sensible et le monde de l'expression. Cours au Collège de France. Notes, 1953*, 92, quoted by S. Kristensen, "Maurice Merleau-Ponty, une esthétique du mouvement,"128. Here Kristensen reminds us that "there is in Bergson an implicit reference to body, but due to the lack of 'a theory of the perceiving body,' he misses the problem of movement 'in the order of phenomena' and he ends up assimilating the divisible duration of the worldly temporality to the duration proper to conscience" (ibid.).

70. M. Merleau-Ponty, *Le monde sensible et le monde de l'expression. Cours au Collège de France. Notes, 1953*, 102.

71. S. Kristensen, "Maurice Merleau-Ponty, une esthétique du mouvement," 129. References to Merleau-Ponty are from M. Merleau-Ponty, *Le monde sensible et le monde de l'expression. Cours au Collège de France. Notes, 1953*, 96.

72. G. Sadoul, *Dictionnaire des Films* (1965), updated by É. Breton (Paris: Seuil, 1976); trans., ed., update, P. Morris, *Dictionary of Films* (Berkeley, Los Angeles: University of California Press, 1972), 430, trans. modified.

73. See M. Merleau-Ponty, *Sense and Non-Sense*, 56.

74. Quoted in G. Sadoul, *Dictionary of Films*, 430.

75. M. Merleau-Ponty, *Le monde sensible et le monde de l'expression. Cours au Collège de France. Notes, 1953*, 119.

76. Ibid., 113.

77. On this subject, Merleau-Ponty writes in his course notes: "perceptual *logos* as such—(the body)" (ibid., 120).

78. M. Merleau-Ponty, "Themes from the Lectures at the Collège de France, 1952–1960," 74.

79. Merleau-Ponty, *Eye and Mind*, 145. I shall refer to the bond between this Merleau-Pontian phrase and the sequence from *Zéro de conduite* as it was exposed in Anna Caterina Dalmasso's article titled "Le medium visible. Interface opaque et immersivité non mimétique," in *Chiasmi* 16 (2014), 109. Further on, the same commentator has bound the Merleau-Pontian similitude of the metaphors by which Jean Epstein describes the effect of slow motion, in a passage of *The Intelligence of a Machine* that Merleau-Ponty quotes in *Le monde sensible et le monde de l'expression: Cours au Collège de France. Notes, 1953*, 116–117. See A. C. Dalmasso, "Le médium visible. Interface opaque et immersivité non mimétique," 116n89.

80. For an inquiry on some "crossings" between Merleau-Ponty's thought and the video-artistic activity of Viola, see I. Matos Dias, *Croisement de regards: La phénoménologie de M. Merleau-Ponty et l'art vidéo de Bill Viola*, *Daímon: Revista de Filosofía* 44 (May–August 2008), 85–92.

81. M. Merleau-Ponty, *Le monde sensible et le monde de l'expression. Cours au Collège de France. Notes*, 1953, 102. In the Introduction to *Signs*, he will write: "the world and Being hold only in movement; it is only in this way that all things can be together" (M. Merleau-Ponty, *Signs*, 22).

82. M. Merleau-Ponty, *Causeries 1948*, established and noted by S. Ménasé (Paris: Seuil, 2002), 57.

83. Ibid., 57–58.

84. Differently from what happened in "The Cinema and The New Psychology" (see M. Merleau-Ponty, *Sense and Non-sense*, 55–56 and 58), the name of André Malraux and his conception of cinema are never quoted in this course's theme and notes. Still, I find it appropriate to point out the convergence between the characterization of cinema as art proposed in this course and what Malraux wrote on this issue in his *Esquisse d'une psychologie du cinéma*, published in 1940 on *Verve* and recalled by Merleau-Ponty precisely in his conference at the IDHEC (indeed, also in the 1948 *Causeries* there are echoes of this article by Malraux). On this issue, Malraux wrote in his article: "So long as the cinema served merely for the portrayal of figures in motion it was no more (and no less) an art than plain photography. Within a defined space, generally a real or imagined theatre stage, actors performed a play or comic scene, which the camera merely recorded. The birth of the cinema as a means of expression (not of reproduction) dates from the abolition of that *defined space*." (A. Malraux, "Esquisse d'une psychologie du

cinéma," in *Verve* 8 (1940); trans. S. K. Langer, "Sketch for a Psychology of the Moving Pictures," in ed. S. K. Langer, *Reflections on Art: A Source Book of Writings by Artists, Critics, and Philosophers* [Baltimore: Johns Hopkins University Press, 1958, 320]). And, a little further, "The means of reproduction in the cinema is the moving photograph, but its means of expression is a sequence of *planes*" (ibid.).

85. M. Merleau-Ponty, *In Praise of Philosophy and Other Essays*, 78 (translation modified).

86. M. Merleau-Ponty, ibid., 79, my emphasis.

87. M. Merleau-Ponty, *Eye and Mind*, 124, my emphasis.

88. A. Bazin, "Ontologie de l'image photographique" [1945], trans. H. Gray, "The Ontology of the Photographic Image," in *Film Quarterly* 13, no. 4 (Summer 1960), 9.

89. M. Merleau-Ponty, *Eye and Mind*, 126.

90. This is what Renaud Barbaras seems to miss when he formulates the following judgment: "Just like Husserl, instead of questioning the subject *starting from* the perceptual relation, Merleau-Ponty tries to *build* the relation starting from a subject whose (empiric-transcendental) bipolarity is not profoundly enquired. The only overcoming with relation to Husserl consists in starting from an embodied subject, rather than from a transcendental subject" (R. Barbaras, *Vie et intentionnalité. Recherches phénoménologiques* [Paris: Vrin, 2003, 156]).

91. M. Merleau-Ponty, *The Visible and the Invisible*, 130.

92. Ibid., 146, my emphasis.

93. Ibid., 152.

94. "If one wants metaphors, it would be better to say that the body sensed and the body sentient are as the obverse and the reverse, or again, as two segments of one sole circular course which goes above from left to right and below from right to left, but which is but one sole movement in its two phases" (ibid., p. 138).

95. M. Merleau-Ponty, *Eye and Mind*, 146.

96. Ibid., 126.

97. Ibid.

98. M. Merleau-Ponty, *The Visible and the Invisible*, 141.

99. See J. L. Godard, *JLG/JLG. Phrases* (Paris: P.O.L., 1996, 69–71).

100. See F. Casetti, *L'occhio del* Novecento. *Cinema, esperienza, modernità* (Milano: Bompiani, 2005); trans. E. Larkin, J. Pranolo, *Eye of the Century: Film, Experience, Modernity* (New York: Columbia University Press, 2008), in particular 162, where on this issue Casetti refers precisely to the reflection of the later Merleau-Ponty. Some of the considerations I propose in the pages that follow are inspired by this book.

101. M. Merleau-Ponty, *Eye and Mind*, 147.

102. Jean Baudrillard will in his turn characterize *simulacra* as *figures of precession*: "it is the map that precedes the territory—*precession of simulacra*—it is the map that engenders the territory" (J. Baudrillard, "La précession des simulacres," in *Simulacres et simulations* [Paris: Galilée, 1981]; trans. P. Foss, P. Patton and P. Beitchman, *Simulations* [New York: Semiotext(e), 1983], 2).

103. As for the occurrences of the word "precession" in Merleau-Ponty's unpublished notes, I shall mark the volume number of the Bibliothèque Nationale de France (BnF), the abbreviation of the unpublished writing, and indicate the BnF numbering for each note's sheet, followed, if any, by Merleau-Ponty's own numbering. Concerning this convention, see E. Saint Aubert, *Du lien des êtres aux éléments de l'être: Merleau-Ponty au tournant des années 1945–1951* (Paris: Vrin, 2004), "Note technique et bibliographique," 9–10.

104. R. Arnheim, *Art and Visual Perception* (Berkeley: University of California Press, 1954). Concerning this occurrence of the word "precession" in Merleau-Ponty's unpublished notes, see BnF, vol. XXI, NL-Arnh [53] (50).

105. These words are respectively translated as "infringement" and "encroachment" in M. Merleau-Ponty, *The Visible and the Invisible*, 134.

106. See BnF, vol. V, OE-ms [36]v(53) and [94](42).

107. BnF, vol. VII, NLVIàf3 [186].

108. BnF, vol. VII, NLVIàf3 [181].

109. Ibid.

110. It is not by chance that the Merleau-Pontian definition of vision that is examined here could be considered as the theoretical core of the convergence between the later Merleau-Ponty and Bazin. Pietro Montani could thus write: "The truth is that Bazin, just like Merleau-Ponty, is a phenomenologist who has seen the ontological stake of imagination: that is, the emergence of the image from an 'ebb' and 'flow,' its constitution as a back and forth of vision from the things to the form and vice-versa, of the data to sense and vice-versa." (P. Montani, *L'immaginazione narrativa. Il racconto del cinema oltre i confini dello spazio letterario* [Milano: Guerini e Associati, 1999], 74).

111. M. Merleau-Ponty, *Eye and Mind*, 147.

112. M. Merleau-Ponty, *The Visible and the Invisible*, 243.

113. Ibid., 24.

114. See G. Didi-Huberman, *Devant le temps. Histoire de l'art et anachronisme des images*, 239–240.

115. M. Merleau-Ponty, *Notes de cours au Collège de France 1958–1959 et 1960–1961*, 115.

116. M. Merleau-Ponty, *Eye and Mind*, 130.

117. See M. Merleau-Ponty, *The Visible and the Invisible*, 149–151.

118. See M. Carbone, *An Unprecedented Deformation. Marcel Proust and the Sensible Ideas.*

119. "Here, on the contrary, there is no vision without the screen: the ideas we are speaking of would not be better known to us if we had no body and no sensibility; it is then that they would be inaccessible to us" (M. Merleau-Ponty, *The Visible and the Invisible*, 150).

120. We might say that that "smile [. . .] keeps producing and reproducing [. . .] on the surface of a canvas" like an image *and at once* like an essence. More precisely, following the expression that Merleau-Ponty uses a few lines below, like a "carnal essence."

121. M. Merleau-Ponty, *Eye and Mind*, 130.

122. Deleuze states something close to this idea in the last answer of the interview given to the *Cahiers du Cinéma*, no. 380, February 1986, when he published *L'image-temps*: "That's funny, because it seems obvious to me that the [cinematic] image is not in the present. What the image 'represents' is in the present, but not the image itself. The image itself is an ensemble of time relations." Then he goes on echoing Proust: "On each occasion, it's 'a little time in the pure state,' and not in the present," (G. Deleuze, "Le cerveau, chest l'écran," in *Cahiers du Cinéma*, no. 380, Février 1986; trans. M. T. Guirgis, "The Brain Is the Screen: An Interview with Gilles Deleuze," in ed. G. Flaxman, *The Brain Is the Screen: Deleuze and the Philosophy of Cinema* [Minneapolis: the University of Minnesota Press, 2000], p. 371, now available also in G. Deleuze, ed. D. Lapoujade, trans. A. Hodges and M. Taormina, *Two regimes of Madness: Texts and Interviews 1975–1995*, rev. ed. [Cambridge, MA: MIT Press, 2007]).

123. One could link the terms of this question also to the struggle of the painter to free his canvas from the "clichés" occupying it even *before* he begins painting. D. H. Lawrence refers to such a struggle, apropos of Cézanne, in a text ("Introduction to These Paintings" [1929]) recalled by Deleuze in his book on Bacon in order to point out that the work of the painter does not consist in reproducing an exterior object, on a *white surface*. See G. Deleuze, *Francis Bacon. Logique de la sensation* [Paris: La différence, 1981]; trans. D. W. Smith, *Francis Bacon: The Logic of Sensation* [Minneapolis, MN: University of Minnesota Press, 2003], 61–62).

124. M. Merleau-Ponty, *In Praise of Philosophy and Other Essays*, 116. According to Deleuze, as we know, it is with the Italian Neorealism movement that "we run [. . .] into a principle of indeterminability, of indiscernibility: we no longer know what is imaginary or real, physical or mental, in the situation, not because they are confused, but because we do not have to know and there is no longer even a place from which to ask. It is as if the real and the imaginary were running after each other, as if each was being reflected in the other, around a point of indiscernibility." (G. Deleuze, *Cinema 2: L'image-temps* [Paris: Minuit, 1985]; trans. H. Tomlinson and R. Galeta, Cinema 2: *The Image-Time* [London: Continuum, 2005]), 7. For putting into a cinematic perspective Deleuze's and Merleau-Ponty's reflections on images, see O. Fahle, "La visibilité du monde: Deleuze, Merleau-Ponty et le cinéma," in ed. A. Beaulieu, *Gilles Deleuze: Héritage Philosophique* (Paris: P.U.F., 2005), 123–143.

125. M. Merleau-Ponty, *Eye and Mind*, 126.

Chapter Five

1. M. Merleau-Ponty, *Notes de cours au Collège de France 1958–1959 et 1960–1961*, 305. For reasons of consistency, I will translate the "Philosophy and Non-Philosophy since Hegel" course notes myself, even if an English translation is available (see M. Merleau-Ponty, "Philosophy and Non-Philosophy Since

Hegel," trans. and ed. Hugh J. Silverman, in *Philosophy and Non-Philosophy Since Merleau-Ponty* [New York and London: Routledge, 1988], 9–83, here 40). —Trans.

2. In the preparatory notes for his 1952–53 course, Merleau-Ponty means to highlight that these two phenomena are "of the same kind" (M. Merleau-Ponty, *Le monde sensible et le monde de l'expression. Cours au Collège de France. Notes, 1953*, 96). See also the following note: "idea that movement = similar to apprehension of figure on ground" (ibid., 95).

3. The Nietzsche concerned here is the one of the "Preface for the Second Edition" (1886) to the *Gay Science*, from which I already quoted, in the second chapter of the present work, a passage that it is useful to recall here in Merleau-Ponty's own French translation: "nous ne croyons plus que la vérité demeure vérité si on lui enlève son *voile*" ["we no longer believe that truth remains truth when the *veils* are withdrawn"] (M. Merleau-Ponty, *Notes de cours au Collège de France 1958–1959 et 1960–1961*, 277, my emphasis). See also the Silverman's English version: M. Merleau-Ponty, "Philosophy and Non-Philosophy Since Hegel," 11.

4. Concerning the search for the traces of "a new idea of light" in Schelling's reflection, which Merleau-Ponty analyses in the first of his three courses on "The Concept of Nature," see F. Moiso, "Una ragione all'altezza della natura. La convergenza fra Schelling e Merleau-Ponty," in *Chiasmi*, N. 1, 1988, 83–90.

5. On this subject, see G. A. Johnson, *The Retrieval of the Beautiful: Thinking Through Merleau-Ponty's Aesthetics*, 107 and ff.

6. R. Delaunay, "La lumière" [1912] now in *Du cubisme à l'art abstrait. Cahiers inédits de R. Delaunay* (Paris: S.E.V.P.E.N., 1957); trans. D. Shapiro and A. A. Cohen, "Light," in ed. A. A. Cohen, *The New Art of Color: The Writings of Robert and Sonia Delaunay* (New York: Viking, 1978), 81.

7. M. Merleau-Ponty, *Eye and Mind*, 142.

8. M. Merleau-Ponty, *Notes de cours au Collège de France 1958–1959 et 1960–1961*, 182.

9. Ibid., 194.

10. For the Proustian pages to which I am referring here and in the following passages, see M. Proust, *Swann's Way*, 334–335.

11. The reader can refer here to my book *La visibilité de l'invisible*, 132 and ff., where I already analyzed the commentary on those pages proposed in *The Visible and the Invisible*.

12. See M. Merleau-Ponty, *The Visible and the Invisible*, 151.

13. M. Merleau-Ponty, *Notes de cours au Collège de France 1958–1959 et 1960–1961*, 194.

14. See ibid.

15. M. Proust, *Swann's Way*, 335.

16. M. Merleau-Ponty, *Notes de cours au Collège de France 1958–1959 et 1960–1961*, 193.

17. Ibid., 196.

18. Ibid.

19. Ibid.

20. Ibid., 195.

21. Ibid., 194.

22. E. Panofsky, *Idea: A Concept in Art Theory*, 31, my emphasis.

23. See note 3 of the present chapter.

24. M. Merleau-Ponty, *Notes de cours au Collège de France 1958–1959 et 1960–1961*, 372.

25. Ibid., 373.

26. M. Merleau-Ponty, *The Visible and the Invisible*, 170. On the reasons for Merleau-Ponty's reference to the distinction between the *logos endiáthetos* and the *logos prophorikós* made by the Jewish philosopher Philo of Alexandria and by Plutarch, and later recalled by the Fathers of the Church, see P. Burke, "La creatività e l'inconscio in Merleau-Ponty e Schelling," in *Chiasmi*, N. 1, 1998, 56 and ff.

27. M. Merleau-Ponty, *Notes de cours au Collège de France 1958–1959 et 1960–1961*, 373.

28. F. Moiso, "Una ragione all'altezza della natura. La convergenza fra Schelling e Merleau-Ponty," 85.

29. Ibid., particularly 83–84.

30. Ibid., 83.

31. See K. Jaspers, *Schelling* (Munchen: Piper, 1955), 291.

32. M. Merleau-Ponty, *Nature*, 42.

33. Ibid., 43.

34. Ibid., 42.

35. F. Moiso, "Una ragione all'altezza della natura. La convergenza fra Schelling e Merleau-Ponty," 85.

36. M. Merleau-Ponty, *Nature*, 42–43.

37. F. Moiso, "Una ragione all'altezza della natura. La convergenza fra Schelling e Merleau-Ponty," 86.

38. H. Trismégiste, *Corpus Hermeticum*, tome I, *Poimandrès*, Traités I–XII, text established by A. D. Nock; trans. A.-J. Festugière (Paris: Les Belles Lettres, 1945), 178.

39. H. Trismegistus, "Poimandres," in ed. and trans., B. P. Copenhaver, *Hermetica* (Cambridge: Cambridge University Press, 1992), 1.

40. Plato, *Timaeus*, ed. and trans. A. E. Taylor (New York: Routledge Library Editions, 2013), 49a, 47.

41. Ibid., 50 c, 49.

42. H. Trismegistus, *Poimandres*, 2.

43. Plato, *Timaeus*, 51 a–b, 50.

44. I owe several aspects of the present interpretation to J.-J. Wunenburger, *Philosophie des images* (Paris: P.U.F., 1997).

45. See above, n7 to Chapter One, 87.

46. M. Merleau-Ponty, *The Visible and the Invisible*, 267.

47. Ibid., 170.

Chapter Six

1. See M. Merleau-Ponty, *Eye and Mind*, 139.

2. See ibid., 132.

3. M. Merleau-Ponty, *Nature*, 204.

4. M. Merleau-Ponty, *Notes de cours au Collège de France 1958–1959 et 1960–1961*, 163.

5. Ibid., 278.

6. F. Nietzsche, *Also sprach Zarathustra. Ein Buch für Alle und Keinen* [1883–1885]; trans. A. del Caro, *Thus Spoke Zarathustra*, ed. A. Del Caro, R. Pippin (Cambridge, UK: Cambridge University Press, 2006), 6.

7. M. Merleau-Ponty, *Notes de cours au Collège de France 1958–1959 et 1960–1961*, 275. On this theme, I shall refer to the second chapter of my book *The Thinking of the Sensible: Merleau-Ponty's A-Philosophy* (Evanston: Northwestern University Press, 2004), 14–27.

8. M. Merleau-Ponty, "The Philosopher and His Shadow," in *Signs*, 160.

9. Ibid.

10. M. Merleau-Ponty, *The Visible and the Invisible*, 149.

11. On this topic, I shall refer also to my book *An Unprecedented Deformation. Marcel Proust and the Sensible Ideas.*

12. M. Merleau-Ponty, *Nature*, 174.

13. M. Merleau-Ponty, *The Visible and the Invisible*, 101, my emphasis.

14. See above, n43 to Chapter Five, 110.

15. "Resemblance subsists, but it is produced as the exterior effect of a simulacrum, inasmuch as it is built upon divergent series and makes them resonate" (G. Deleuze, *The Logic of Sense*, 262).

16. M. Merleau-Ponty, *The Visible and the Invisible*, 152.

17. See G. Deleuze, *The Fold: Leibniz and the Baroque*, 8.

18. P. Claudel, "Traité de la Co-naissance au monde et de soi-même," in *Art pratique* [1907] (Paris: Gallimard, 1984); trans. R. Spodheim, "Discourse on the Affinity with the World and On Oneself," in *Poetic Art* (New York: Philosophical Library, 1948), 40. On this issue, see in particular E. de Saint Aubert, "La 'co-naissance.' Merleau-Ponty et Claudel," in eds. M. Cariou, R. Barbaras, E. Bimbenet, *Merleau-Ponty aux frontières de l'invisible*, Cahier de "Chiasmi International," N. 1 (Milano: Mimesis, 2003), 249–277.

19. M. Merleau-Ponty, *The Visible and the Invisible*, 221.

20. In this sense, it seems to me that we can interpret the commentary of Merleau-Ponty apropos of an observation of Claude Simon: "The decision is not *ex nihilo*, is not now, always anticipated, because we are everything, everything is complicit in us. We decide to do nothing but rather to let be" (M. Merleau-Ponty, *Notes de cours au Collège de France 1958–1959 et 1960–1961*, 214).

21. M. Merleau-Ponty, *Nature*, 283.

22. G. Deleuze, "Sur Nietzsche et l'image de la pensée" [1968], now in *L'île deserte. Textes et entretiens 1953–1974* (Paris: Minuit, 2002); trans. M. Taormina, "On Nietzsche and the Image of Thought," in *Desert Islands and Other Texts* (Cambridge: MIT Press, 2003), 139. "The Image of Thought" is the title of the "Conclusion" to the first edition of *Marcel Proust et les signes* [1964] (Paris: P.U.F., 1998); trans. R. Howard, *Proust and Signs* (London: Athlone, 2000). It is also the title of a chapter of *Difference et répetition* [1968] (Paris: P.U.F., 2009); trans. P. Patton, *Difference and Repetition* (London: Athlone, 1994), 129 and ff.

23. G. Deleuze, *Desert Islands and Other Texts*, 193.

24. On this point, another reference to Proust's novel can serve as an example: in the first volume of the series, he describes three executions of the imaginary sonata of Vinteuil, to each of which he connects different historical sources of inspiration. It seems, then, legitimate to ask where its identity resides. On this, I refer the reader to my "Composing Vinteuil: Proust's Unheard Music," trans. D. Jacobson, *Res* 48 (2005), 163–165. There is an evident convergence between the present reflections and those that Jean-Luc Nancy developed in *À l'écoute* (Paris, Galilée 2002).

25. M. Merleau-Ponty, *The Visible and the Invisible*, 266.

26. Ibid.

27. For a reflection on the history of the reception of this anecdote and on its relevance, see H. Blumenberg, *Das Lachen der Trakerin: Eine Urgeschichte der Theorie* (Frankfurt am Main: Suhrkamp, 1987). For other reflections on this point, see also A. Cavarero, *Nonostante Platone: Figure femminili nella filosofia antica* (Rome: Editori uniti, 1990); trans. S. Anderlini-D'Onofrio, *In Spite of Plato: A Feminist Rewriting of Ancient Philosophy* (New York: Routledge, 1995).

28. M. Merleau-Ponty, *Notes de cours au Collège de France 1958–1959 et 1960–1961*, 275.

Index